BASIC ACCOUNTING

Series editor
Brian Coyle

PASSWORD BASIC ACCOUNTING

First edition July 1989

ISBN 1 871824 02 8

Published by
BPP Publishing Ltd
BPP House, Aldine Place,
142/144 Uxbridge Road, London W12 8AA

Printed by Dotesios Printers Ltd, Trowbridge

A CIP Catalogue reference for this book
is available from the British Library

Copyright © 1989 BPP Publishing Ltd

CONTENTS

	Page
Preface.	v
How to use this book.	vi

SECTION 1: NOTES AND QUESTIONS	Page	SECTION 2: MARKING SCHEDULES AND COMMENTS	Page
1. Introduction.	3	. . . .	157
2. Ledger accounting.	13	. . . .	161
3. Adjustments to accounts.	25	. . . .	167
4. Fixed assets and depreciation.	39	. . . .	173
5. Accounting for stocks.	49	. . . .	179
6. Control accounts and bank reconciliations.	61	. . . .	185
7. Incomplete records.	75	. . . .	193
8. Income and expenditure accounts.	85	. . . .	199
9. Manufacturing accounts.	95	. . . .	205
10. Partnership accounts.	105	. . . .	211
11. Company accounts.	119	. . . .	217
12. Funds statements.	131	. . . .	223
13. Accounting ratios.	143	. . . .	231

PREFACE

PASSWORD is a series of multiple choice question books on business and accountancy topics. If you are studying for an examination, or would just like to test your knowledge on one of these topics, Password books have two special features which are designed to help you.

1 They contain about 300 multiple choice questions, with answers provided later in the book. You can get an objective idea of your strengths and weaknesses, and whether your standard is as high as you would like it to be.

2 We explain most solutions in some detail, to show why one answer is correct and the others are wrong. Our comments should help you to learn from any mistakes you have made, and to improve your understanding of the subject.

Objective testing is an increasingly popular method of examination. An answer is right or wrong, and there are no 'grey areas' or 'in-between answers' that are half-right or arguably correct. Multiple choice questions (MCQs) are the form of objective testing that is now most widely used. Professional bodies that have adopted MCQs for some examination papers include the Institute of Chartered Accountants in England and Wales, the Institute of Chartered Accountants of Scotland and the Chartered Institute of Management Accountants. The Chartered Association of Certified Accountants has recently taken a first step in the same direction.

MCQs offer much more than exam practice, though. They test your knowledge and understanding. And they help with learning.

- The brevity of the questions, and having to select a correct answer from four choices (A, B, C or D) makes them convenient to use. You can do some on your journey to or from work or college on the train or the bus.

- We know from experience that many people like MCQs, find them fun and enjoy the opportunity to mark their own answers exactly.

- Being short, MCQs are able collectively to cover every aspect of a topic area. They make you realise what you know and what you don't.

If you're looking for the fun and challenge of self-testing, or preparing for an examination - not just a multiple choice exam - Password is designed to help you. You can check your own standard, monitor your progress, spot your own weaknesses, and learn things that you hadn't picked up from your text-book or study manual. Most important, Password books allow you to find out for yourself just how good you are at a topic, and whether you still need to do some more work to reach the target that you have set for yourself.

Good luck!

Brian Coyle
July 1989

PASSWORD. MULTIPLE CHOICE

HOW TO USE THIS BOOK

Aims of the book

This book is designed:

- to familiarise you with a type of question that you are increasingly likely to face if you are studying for examinations

- to develop your knowledge of Basic Accounting through repeated practice on questions covering all areas of the subject. There are more than 300 questions in this book.

The multiple choice approach

A multiple choice question is in two parts.

- The *stem* sets out the problem or task to be solved. It may be in the form of a question, or it may be an unfinished statement which has to be completed.

- The *options* are the possible responses from which you must choose the one you believe to be correct. There is only one correct option (called the *key*); the other, incorrect, options are called *distractors*.

There are various ways in which you may be asked to indicate your chosen response. If you meet with MCQs in an examination, you should obviously read the instructions carefully. In this book, you will find that the options are identified by the letters A, B, C, D. To indicate your choice, draw a circle round the letter you have chosen.

The notes

In Section 1 of this book each chapter begins with brief notes which are designed to refresh your memory of the subject area and get you thinking along the right lines before you begin to tackle the questions.

The notes are *not* a substitute for a textbook: Password assumes that you are already broadly familiar with the topics covered in the chapter. Nor do they give you answers to all the questions.

- The notes are a *reminder* of the key points in each topic area. If your studies have left you feeling that you can't see the wood for the trees, the notes may help to bring the important issues into focus.

- They provide brief *guidance* on particularly knotty points or areas which often cause problems for students.

- Finally, they set out any *conventions* that are to be adopted in the questions. For example, there are numerous equally valid methods of calculating a gearing ratio. But this kind of ambiguity is fatal to a successful MCQ. For this reason, you will find that the notes to chapter 13 specify which ratio is to be used. This does not mean that other ratios are inferior: only that this book, in the interests of clarity, adopts one method rather than any other.

The questions

The questions are arranged roughly in the order of the key areas highlighted by the notes. But it is difficult, and undesirable, to keep topics completely separate: there's a great deal of overlapping.

The general principle has been for questions *on each topic* to get progressively harder. The result of this is that within a single chapter the level of difficulty will rise, and then fall back to begin rising again. So if you have trouble with two or three questions, don't assume that you have to give up on the whole chapter: there may be easier questions ahead!

Try to work through a whole chapter before turning to the solutions. If you refer to the marking schedule after each question you will find it almost impossible to avoid seeing the answer to the next question, and the value of the book will be lessened.

Finally, don't rush your answers. Distractors are exactly what their name suggests: they are meant to look plausible and distract you from the correct option. Unless you are absolutely certain you know the answer, look carefully at each option in turn before making your choice. There is enough blank space on each page for any rough workings that may be necessary. You should not need writing paper or any other aids beyond a pen and a calculator.

The marking schedules

The marking schedules indicate the correct answer to each question and the number of marks available. You should add up the marks on all the questions you got right and compare your total with the maximum marks available.

At the foot of each marking schedule there is a rating, which is intended to be helpful in indicating the amount of work you still need to do on each topic. You'll need to use your discretion in interpreting your rating, though. The book may be used by a very wide range of readers, from GCSE students, through students of college or professional business and accountancy courses, to qualified accounts personnel with years of practical experience. A mark of 10 out of 35 might be worryingly low for an experienced accountant, while representing a very creditable achievement for someone at an earlier stage of his studies.

The comments

The answers to purely factual questions generally need no explanation, but for others there is a commentary, often very detailed.

These comments will usually describe why a particular option is correct or set out the calculations leading to the correct answer. Distractors are usually chosen to illustrate common misconceptions, or plausible, but incorrect, lines of calculation. The comments will often highlight what is wrong about particular distractors and this should help in clarifying your ideas about topics that you may have misunderstood.

Conclusion

Password Basic Accounting is designed as an aid both to learning and to revision. It is not primarily aimed at those who are already expert in the subject. So don't expect to score 100%. And don't despair if your marks seem relatively low. Choosing the wrong answer to a question is not a failure, if by studying the solution and comments you learn something you did not know before. This is particularly relevant if you are using the book at an early stage in your studies, rather than in the final stages of revision.

And if you *do* score 100%? There are 14 other Password titles to get through...

SECTION 1

NOTES AND QUESTIONS

CHAPTER 1

INTRODUCTION TO ACCOUNTING

> This chapter covers the following topics:
> - The purpose of accounting
> - Accounting concepts
> - The accounting equation
> - Introduction to the balance sheet and profit and loss account

1. The purpose of accounting

1.1 Accounts are prepared because:

- most businesses are continuous, but periodic reports are needed to assess whether their trading activities are successful or not;

- many businesses are managed by people other than their owners. The owners will wish to see how well their managers are performing;

- accounting information can play an important role in the running of a business. For example, a record of goods sold is essential to a proper system of credit control.

1.2 *The corporate report* is an important document in this context. It identifies a number of categories of people who may be interested in accounting information, and a number of characteristics that such information should possess.

Users of accounting information	Characteristics of useful information
Equity investors	Relevant
Loan creditors	Understandable
Employees	Reliable
Analysts and advisors	Complete
Business contacts	Objective
The government	Timely
The public	Comparable

1: INTRODUCTION TO ACCOUNTING

2. Accounting concepts

2.1 SSAP 2 *Disclosure of accounting policies* identifies four *fundamental accounting concepts:* going concern, accruals, consistency, prudence.

2.2 The Companies Act 1985 identifies five *accounting principles.* They are the same as the SSAP 2 concepts, with the addition of the *separate valuation principle.*

2.3 A number of other concepts have been identified as important by authors on accounting. Although there is no agreed list, the most common are probably: the entity concept; the money measurement concept; and the materiality concept.

Do you know what each of these is?

3. The accounting equation

3.1 Accountants regard a business as an entity separate from its owners. Under this convention, capital can be regarded as being on a par with liabilities in business accounts, because it is 'owed' by the business to its owners.

3.2 The *accounting equation* is based on this idea. It states that for any business, and at any time:

$$\boxed{\text{Capital} + \text{Liabilities} = \text{Assets}}$$

3.3 Profits (P) are an addition to business capital. Capital may also be increased by a new injection of funds (C_i) from the owners. Capital is reduced by drawings (D), being withdrawals of funds by the owners. The increase (I) in a business's net assets over a period depends on these three factors, and can be calculated by the following equation:

$$\boxed{I = P + C_i - D}$$

3.4 It is usual to re-arrange this relationship to provide a formula for calculating the profit (P) made by a business during a period:

$$\boxed{P = I + D - C_i}$$

This is *the business equation.*

4. Introduction to the balance sheet and profit and loss account

4.1 A *balance sheet* is a list of the assets, liabilities and capital of a business at a given moment.

4.2 Fixed assets are assets held by a business over more than one accounting period. They are depreciated over their useful lives so as to spread their cost over the accounting periods which benefit from their use.

4.3 Current assets are cash and other assets which will soon be converted into cash in the course of the business's normal trade.

4.4 Assets are financed (and matched in the balance sheet) by capital and liabilities. Liabilities may be current (eg normal trade creditors) or long-term (eg a debenture loan).

4.5 A *profit and loss account* matches the revenue earned in a period with the costs incurred in earning it. It is usual to distinguish between a gross profit (sales revenue less the cost of goods sold) and a net profit (being the gross profit less the expenses of selling, distribution, administration etc).

4.6 Another important distinction is between capital expenditure and revenue expenditure.

- *Capital expenditure* is expenditure on fixed assets and is included in the balance sheet of the business.

- *Revenue expenditure* is charged in the profit and loss account and relates to the running costs of the business.

1: INTRODUCTION TO ACCOUNTING

QUESTIONS

1 What is *The corporate report?*

A A discussion paper published by the Accounting Standards Committee

B A statement of recommended practice published by the Accounting Standards Committee

C A statement of standard accounting practice published by the Accounting Standards Committee

D A proposed revision of the law relating to company accounts published by the government

Circle your answer

A   B   C   D

2 *The corporate report* identifies seven categories of people having a right to financial information about companies. Which one of the following is *not* included in the list?

A Trade contacts
B Financial analysts
C The general public
D Managers of the company

Circle your answer

A   B   C   D

3 *The corporate report* identifies seven characteristics of useful information. Which one of the following is *not* included in the list?

A Simplicity
B Comparability
C Reliability
D Completeness

Circle your answer

A   B   C   D

4 Which one of the following accounting concepts is *not* one of the fundamental concepts identified in SSAP 2?

A The going concern concept
B The consistency concept
C The prudence concept
D The entity concept

Circle your answer

A   B   C   D

1: INTRODUCTION TO ACCOUNTING

5 A company owns an item of stock which cost £4 and has a net realisable value of £3. The company accountant is unsure which of these valuations to use in preparing a balance sheet. Which of the following concepts should dictate his choice?

    A The going concern concept
    B The accruals concept
    C The prudence concept
    D The money measurement concept

Circle your answer

A   B   C   D

6 Andy starts a business and introduces capital of £10,000. He also obtains a loan of £6,000 to purchase fixed assets.

The amount of his opening net assets is:

    A £4,000
    B £6,000
    C £10,000
    D £16,000

Circle your answer

A   B   C   D

7 A trader's net profit for the year may be computed by using which of the following formulae?

    A Opening capital + drawings - capital introduced - closing capital

    B Closing capital + drawings - capital introduced - opening capital

    C Opening capital - drawings + capital introduced - closing capital

    D Closing capital - drawings + capital introduced - opening capital

Circle your answer

A   B   C   D

8 The profit earned by a business in 19X7 was £72,500. The proprietor injected new capital of £8,000 during the year and withdrew goods for his private use which had cost £2,200.

If net assets at the beginning of 19X7 were £101,700, what were the closing net assets?

    A £35,000
    B £39,400
    C £168,400
    D £180,000

Circle your answer

A   B   C   D

1: INTRODUCTION TO ACCOUNTING

9 The profit made by a business in 19X7 was £35,400. The proprietor injected new capital of £10,200 during the year and withdrew a monthly salary of £500.

If net assets at the end of 19X7 were £95,100, what was the proprietor's capital at the beginning of the year?

A £50,000
B £55,500
C £63,900
D £134,700

Circle your answer

A   B   C   D

10 A business had net assets of £32,500 at 1 January 19X9. The net profit, after proprietor's drawings, for the year ended 31 December 19X9 was £13,250. Drawings were made at the rate of £750 per month in cash. The proprietor also withdrew for his own use goods costing £340 and with a selling price of £800. No new capital was introduced during the year.

What were the net assets at 31 December 19X9?

A £35,950
B £36,410
C £45,750
D £64,430

Circle your answer

A   B   C   D

11 A business had net assets at 1 January and 31 December 19X9 of £75,600 and £73,800 respectively. During the year, the proprietor introduced additional capital of £17,700 and withdrew cash and goods to the value of £16,300.

What profit or loss was made by the business in 19X9?

A £3,200 loss
B £400 loss
C £400 profit
D £3,200 profit

Circle your answer

A   B   C   D

12 A business had net assets at 1 January and 31 December 19X9 of £47,100 and £54,200 respectively. During the year the proprietor introduced additional capital of £22,000 and made drawings of £200 per week.

What profit or loss was made by the business in 19X9?

A £18,700 loss
B £4,500 loss
C £4,500 profit
D £18,700 profit

Circle your answer

A   B   C   D

8

1: INTRODUCTION TO ACCOUNTING

13 The net profit earned by a business in the year ended 31 December 19X9 was £8,500. Balance sheets of the business at 1 January and 31 December 19X9 showed net assets of £84,300 and £92,500 respectively. The proprietor made regular cash drawings of £150 per month and also withdrew goods for his own use on several occasions during the year. On 30 September he had a pools win and put the whole of his winnings into the business as new capital.

Calculate the amount by which the cost of *goods* withdrawn by the proprietor exceeds or falls short of the amount of his pools win.

A Goods withdrawn exceed pools winnings by £300

B Goods withdrawn exceed pools winnings by £1,500

C Goods withdrawn fall short of pools winnings by £300

D Goods withdrawn fall short of pools winnings by £1,500

Circle your answer

A   B   C   D

14 The net profit earned by a business in the year ended 30 September 19X9 was £10,600. Balance sheets of the business as at 1 October 19X8 and 30 September 19X9 showed net assets of £183,400 and £169,700 respectively. The proprietor withdrew goods costing £2,800 for his own use during the year. He also withdrew a regular amount of cash to cover living expenses and injected new cash when he inherited funds from a deceased relative.

Calculate the amount by which total *cash* drawings exceed or fall short of the new capital injected.

A Cash drawings exceed new capital by £24,300

B Cash drawings exceed new capital by £21,500

C Cash drawings fall short of new capital by £3,100

D Cash drawings fall short of new capital by £5,900

Circle your answer

A   B   C   D

1: INTRODUCTION TO ACCOUNTING

15 Which one of the following costs would be classified as capital expenditure in the accounts of a business?

A The annual depreciation charge on freehold premises

B The cost of redecorating freehold premises

C The cost of roof repairs on freehold premises

D Solicitors' fees in connection with the acquisition of freehold premises

Circle your answer

A   B   C   D

16 Which one of the following items should be treated as capital expenditure in the accounts of a sole trader?

A £2,000 spent on purchasing a micro-computer for re-sale

B £700 drawings to buy a new television for the proprietor

C £200 spent on purchasing a new typewriter to replace his secretary's old one

D £150 paid to a painter in respect of office decoration

Circle your answer

A   B   C   D

17 Which one of the following costs would be classified as revenue expenditure on the invoice for a new company car?

A Road tax
B Number plates
C Fitted stereo radio
D Delivery costs

Circle your answer

A   B   C   D

10

1: INTRODUCTION TO ACCOUNTING

18 A business purchased a machine at a cost of £8,300 including £200 carriage from the supplier's premises and £300 installation costs. After two months in operation the machine broke down and cost £450 to repair. In the balance sheet at the year end the asset's cost would appear as:

- A £8,000
- B £8,100
- C £8,300
- D £8,750

Circle your answer

A   B   C   D

19 Which one of the following assets may be classified as an intangible fixed asset in the accounts of a business?

- A Leasehold premises
- B Trade investment
- C Goodwill
- D Preliminary expenses of incorporation

Circle your answer

A   B   C   D

20 Which one of the following would *not* be classified amongst current liabilities in the accounts of a business?

- A A provision for doubtful debts
- B Accrued interest charges
- C Bank overdraft
- D Corporation tax payable

Circle your answer

A   B   C   D

21 Which one of the following expenses would normally be shown in the trading account of a business?

- A Carriage outwards
- B Carriage inwards
- C Warehousing costs
- D Bad debts written off

Circle your answer

A   B   C   D

22 What is the correct treatment of bad debts recovered in the trading and profit and loss account of a business?

- A A credit in the trading account
- B A charge in the trading account
- C A credit in the profit and loss account
- D A charge in the profit and loss account

Circle your answer

A   B   C   D

CHAPTER 2

LEDGER ACCOUNTING

> This chapter covers the following topics:
>
> - Books of prime entry
> - Double entry and ledger accounts
> - Ledger accounting for bills of exchange
> - Ledger accounting for VAT

1. Books of prime entry

1.1 Books of prime entry are so called because they are the books of account in which business transactions are initially logged. They include:

- *The cash book* - which records cash and cheques received or paid out by the business
- *The petty cash book* - which records cash expenditure on small items
- *The sales day book* - which records sales invoices despatched to customers
- *The purchase day book* - which records purchase invoices received from suppliers
- *The sales returns day book* - which records goods returned by customers
- *The purchase returns day book* - which records goods returned to suppliers
- *The journal* - which records unusual movements between ledger accounts, arising outside the normal system of postings.

1.2 The purpose of books of prime entry is to 'capture' accounting transactions as they take place. For example, as soon as a sales invoice is raised, it is entered in the sales day book with details of the customer, the date and the amount due. Similar details are recorded in the purchase day book as soon as invoices are received from suppliers.

1.3 Books of prime entry are not themselves part of the double entry system. But they are the source of postings to the ledger accounts which make up the nominal ledger and subsidiary ledgers.

2. Double entry and ledger accounts

2.1 Double entry bookkeeping is based on the same idea as the accounting equation. Every accounting transaction alters the make-up of a business's assets and liabilities. But because the equality of assets and liabilities is always preserved, it follows that each transaction must have two equal but opposite effects.

2: LEDGER ACCOUNTING

2.2 In a system of double entry bookkeeping every accounting event must be entered in ledger accounts both as a debit and as an equal but opposite credit. The principal accounts are contained in a ledger called the nominal ledger.

2.3 Some accounts in the nominal ledger represent the total of very many smaller balances. For example, the debtors account represents all the balances owed by individual customers of the business, while the creditors account represents all amounts owed by the business to its suppliers.

2.4 To keep track of individual customer and supplier balances, it is common to maintain subsidiary ledgers (called the sales ledger and the purchase ledger respectively). Each account in these ledgers represents the balance owed by or to an individual customer or supplier. These subsidiary ledgers are kept purely for reference and are therefore known as *memorandum* records. They do *not* normally form part of the double entry system.

2.5 The rules of double entry bookkeeping are best learnt by considering the cash book. In the cash book a *credit* entry indicates a payment made by the business; the matching debit entry is then made in an account denoting an expense paid, an asset purchased or a liability settled. A *debit* entry in the cash book indicates cash received by the business; the matching credit entry is then made in an account denoting revenue received, a liability created or an asset realised.

2.6 At suitable intervals, the entries in each ledger account are totalled and a balance is struck. Balances are usually collected in a trial balance which is then used as a basis for preparing a profit and loss account and a balance sheet.

3. Ledger accounting for bills of exchange

3.1 Mr Broke owes £400 to Mr Flush. Mr Flush prepares a document in which Mr Broke acknowledges his debt. Mr Broke signs the document to indicate his agreement and returns it to Mr Flush.

3.2 This is the process of drawing a bill of exchange.

- Mr Flush has drawn the bill and is called the drawer.
- Mr Broke has, by his signature, accepted the bill and is called the acceptor or drawee.

3.3 A bill of exchange is a *negotiable instrument*. The meaning of this term is that a bill can be transferred from one holder to another, and the new holder is then entitled to receive the money payable by the drawee. For example, Mr Flush may, if he wishes, sell the bill of exchange to his bank. The result of this process (known as *discounting* the bill) is that Mr Flush receives funds immediately from the bank, while the bank becomes entitled to receive the £400 from Mr Broke on the due date.

3.4 A bank will wish to make a profit on such transactions and will do so by buying the bill from Mr Flush for less than its face value of £400.

3.5 On the due date, the holder of the bill will present it for payment to Mr Broke. If Mr Broke refuses to pay he is said to *dishonour* the bill. The holder of the bill will then (usually) have a claim for his money against the previous holder. For example, if Mr Flush has discounted the bill with a bank, and the bank cannot recover the money from Mr Broke, it will require Mr Flush instead to pay the full £400.

3.6 In ledger accounts, a bill of exchange payable by a business is similar to a creditor balance; a bill of exchange receivable is similar to a debtor balance.

4. Ledger accounting for VAT

4.1 Businesses which are registered for VAT charge tax on the goods they sell to customers. They are obliged to hand over the VAT collected in this way to Customs and Excise. VAT collected from customers is therefore a liability in the accounts of a business.

4.2 Businesses will also be *payers* of VAT, because they will purchase supplies of various kinds on which VAT is charged by the suppliers. Provided that they are VAT-registered, such businesses are entitled to reclaim from Customs and Excise the VAT they have paid. VAT paid on purchases is therefore an asset in the accounts of a business.

4.3 The net amount owed by the business (VAT collected on sales less VAT suffered on purchases) must be calculated every three months and paid over to Customs and Excise.

4.4 The standard rate of VAT is currently 15% of the net price. However, some goods are taxable at the rate of zero per cent. A business which sells such goods will clearly be collecting no VAT from its customers and therefore will have no VAT liability in its books. In fact, because it can still reclaim the tax paid on its own purchases, there will be an amount *recoverable* from Customs and Excise appearing as a debtor in the accounts.

4.5 Some services supplied by businesses are *exempt* from VAT. This means that no VAT is charged on sales, but no VAT can be reclaimed on purchases.

4.6 It is worth noting two particular cases where VAT paid by a business cannot be recovered: the VAT paid on company cars and on entertaining expenses is *never* recoverable, even by a business whose sales are all taxable.

2: LEDGER ACCOUNTING

QUESTIONS

1 Which one of the following records is *not* a book of prime entry?

- A Bank statements
- B Petty cash book
- C Journal
- D Sales returns day book

Circle your answer

A   B   C   D

2 Which one of the following records is often maintained on an imprest system?

- A Cash book
- B Petty cash book
- C Journal
- D Sales day book

Circle your answer

A   B   C   D

3 Which one of the following records might form part of a business's double entry accounting system?

- A Sales ledger
- B Sales day book
- C Sales returns day book
- D Journal

Circle your answer

A   B   C   D

4 The extract below is taken from a book of prime entry.

Date	Narrative	Folio	Total £	Discounts allowed £	Sales ledger £	Sundry £
1.5.19X9	M James & Co	SL12	140.00	10.00	140.00	-

Which book of prime entry is represented here?

- A Sales day book
- B Purchase day book
- C Journal
- D Cash book

Circle your answer

A   B   C   D

16

2: LEDGER ACCOUNTING

5 What ledger entries would be made to record the purchase of an item of machinery on credit?

- A Debit machinery, credit cash
- B Debit machinery, credit creditors
- C Debit purchases, credit creditors
- D Debit creditors, credit machinery

Circle your answer

A   B   C   D

6 What transaction is represented by the entries: debit bank, credit M Smith?

- A Sale of goods to Smith for cash
- B Purchase of goods from Smith for cash
- C Receipt of cash from Smith
- D Payment of cash to Smith

Circle your answer

A   B   C   D

7 What ledger entries would be made to record cash withdrawn by the business proprietor for his personal use?

- A Debit capital, credit drawings
- B Debit cash, credit drawings
- C Debit drawings, credit capital
- D Debit drawings, credit cash

Circle your answer

A   B   C   D

8 What transaction is represented by the entries: debit rent, credit landlord?

- A The receipt of rental income by the business
- B The issue of an invoice for rent to a tenant
- C The payment of rent by the business
- D The receipt of a bill for rent payable by the business

Circle your answer

A   B   C   D

9 What ledger entries would be made to record goods withdrawn by the business proprietor for his personal use?

- A Debit drawings, credit purchases
- B Debit purchases, credit drawings
- C Debit capital, credit drawings
- D Debit purchases, credit sales

Circle your answer

A   B   C   D

17

2: LEDGER ACCOUNTING

10 Which one of the following occurrences could *not* account for a credit balance on a trade debtor's account?

A A sales invoice has been paid twice
B A sales invoice has been posted to another customer's account in error
C Returns outwards have not been taken into account
D A cheque from the customer was made out in the wrong amount

Circle your answer

A   B   C   D

11 Customer Ltd receives goods from Supplier Ltd on credit. Subsequently, payment is made by cheque. It then becomes apparent that the goods are faulty. This is discovered just in time for Customer Ltd to cancel the cheque before it can be cashed.

What entries should be made by Customer Ltd to record the cancellation of the cheque?

A Debit returns outwards, credit creditors
B Debit creditors, credit returns outwards
C Debit creditors, credit bank
D Debit bank, credit creditors

Circle your answer

A   B   C   D

12 What transaction is represented by the entries: debit bank, credit cash?

A Topping up of the petty cash imprest balance
B Payment of bank charges
C Receipt from credit customer paying by cash
D Lodgement of cash in the bank

Circle your answer

A   B   C   (D)

13 The returns outwards book is totalled at convenient intervals and the total must be entered into appropriate ledger accounts. Which one of the following postings would be acceptable?

A Debit returns outwards, credit creditors
B Debit creditors, credit purchases
C Debit returns outwards, credit debtors
D Debit sales, credit debtors

Circle your answer

A   B   C   D

18

2: LEDGER ACCOUNTING

14 Expenses recorded in the petty cash book are posted:

A to the credit of the suppliers' personal accounts

B to the credit of the nominal ledger expense accounts

C to the debit of the nominal ledger expense accounts

D to the debit of the main cash book

Circle your answer

| A | B | C | D |

15 Which one of the following occurrences might explain the existence of a credit balance on an individual debtor's account?

A The bookkeeper failed to make a posting from the returns inwards book to the debtors ledger

B The debtor took advantage of a settlement discount and paid less than the full amount invoiced

C The bookkeeper failed to post an invoice from the sales day book to the debtors ledger

D The bookkeeper posted a total from the returns inwards book to the debtors control account twice by mistake

Circle your answer

| A | B | C | D |

16 Flintstone Ltd accepts a bill of exchange drawn by Rubble Ltd to cover the cost of goods supplied for resale. What entries should be made in the books of Flintstone?

A Debit purchases, credit trade creditors

B Debit purchases, credit bills of exchange payable

C Debit bills of exchange receivable, credit sales

D Debit bills of exchange receivable, credit debtors

Circle your answer

| A | B | C | D |

2: LEDGER ACCOUNTING

17 England Ltd exports goods valued at £2,700 to Gambia Ltd. Gambia Ltd has accepted a bill of exchange in that amount. What entries must England Ltd make to record the bill?

A Debit bank, credit bills of exchange receivable

B Debit debtors, credit bills of exchange receivable

C Debit trade debtors, credit sales

D Debit bills of exchange receivable, credit sales

Circle your answer

A   B   C   D

18 Start plc supplies goods to Middle Ltd on ordinary credit terms and records the sale correctly in its books of account. Middle Ltd draws a bill of exchange which is accepted by End & Co. Middle Ltd endorses the bill over to Start plc in settlement of the outstanding debt. What entries should now be made in the books of Start plc?

A Debit bills of exchange receivable, credit debtors

B Debit debtors, credit bills of exchange receivable

C Debit creditors, credit bills of exchange payable

D Debit bills of exchange payable, credit debtors

Circle your answer

A   B   C   D

19 A trader draws a bill of exchange for £1,200 which is accepted by a credit customer. The trader immediately discounts the bill with his bank, incurring discounting charges of 5%. Which of the following entries correctly describes the outcome of these transactions, in the books of the trader?

A Debit creditors £1,140, debit discounting charges £60, credit debtors £1,200

B Debit debtors £1,140, debit discounting charges £60, credit bank £1,200

C Debit bank £1,200, credit debtors £1,140, credit discounting charges £60

D Debit bank £1,140, debit discounting charges £60, credit debtors £1,200

Circle your answer

A   B   C   D

2: LEDGER ACCOUNTING

20 Goody draws a bill of exchange, accepted by Baddy, in settlement of an outstanding trading balance of £4,000. Goody discounts the bill with his bankers, incurring charges of 3%. All these transactions have been correctly recorded in Goody's books.

When the bill is presented for payment, Baddy is found to be bankrupt. What accounting entries should Goody now make?

A *Debit* Bad debts a/c   £4,000
   Credit Bank a/c   £4,000

B *Debit* Bad debts a/c   £4,000
   Credit Debtors control a/c   £4,000

C *Debit* Bad debts a/c   £4,000
   Credit Bills receivable a/c   £4,000

D *Debit* Discount charges a/c £120
   Debit Bad debts a/c   £3,880
   Credit Creditors a/c   £4,000

Circle your answer

A   B   C   D

21 Den and Angie are an import/export business in London's East End. Most of their customers pay by cheque or banker's draft but for certain customers they have agreed to accept payment by means of a bill of exchange.

The following transactions relate to the bills of exchange receivable account for the month of March 19X8.

March 1   Opening balance £28,500
March 12 Dirty Ltd accepted a 3 month bill for £12,000
March 19 Den and Angie's bank notified them that a bill from Flyboys Ltd for £10,000 which had been discounted with the bank in February at $2\frac{1}{2}$% had been dishonoured on presentation
March 21 A bill of exchange receivable from Safesure Ltd for £6,750 was honoured on presentation
March 31 The bill from Dirty Ltd was discounted with the bank. Discounting charges incurred were £350

At close of business on 31 March 19X8 the balance on Den and Angie's bills of exchange receivable account would be:

A £21,750
B £22,100
C £28,500
D £31,750

Circle your answer

A   B   C   D

2: LEDGER ACCOUNTING

22 Sellbridges Ltd, a retail store whose sales are all on cash terms and are all subject to VAT at the standard rate, receive cash takings from customers of £60,720 in a particular week.

How much VAT is due to Customs and Excise?

A £5,520
B £6,072
C £7,920
D £9,108

Circle your answer

A   B   C   D

23 During the first quarter of 19X9 a business had taxable outputs, net of VAT, of £42,780 and taxable inputs, net of VAT, of £30,360. All are subject to VAT at standard rate. At the end of the quarter, how much VAT is payable or recoverable from Customs and Excise?

A £1,863 payable
B £1,863 recoverable
C £1,620 payable
D £1,620 recoverable

Circle your answer

A   B   C   D

24 A business purchases machinery on credit for £13,800, inclusive of VAT at the standard rate. What accounting entries are needed to reflect this transaction?

A   *Debit*   Machinery   £13,800
    Credit Creditors   £13,800

B   *Debit*   Machinery   £13,800
    Credit VAT   £1,800
    Credit Creditors   £12,000

C   *Debit*   Machinery   £12,000
    Debit   VAT   £1,800
    Credit Creditors   £13,800

D   *Debit*   Machinery   £13,800
    Debit   VAT   £2,070
    Credit Creditors   £15,870

Circle your answer

A   B   C   D

2: LEDGER ACCOUNTING

25 A business purchases a motor car on credit for one of its salesmen. The cost is £9,200 plus VAT. What accounting entries are needed to reflect this transaction?

A	*Debit*	Motor cars	£9,200	
	Credit	Creditors		£9,200
B	*Debit*	Motor cars	£10,580	
	Credit	Creditors		£10,580
C	*Debit*	Motor cars	£9,200	
	Debit	VAT	£1,380	
	Credit	Creditors		£10,580
D	*Debit*	Motor cars	£10,580	
	Credit	VAT		£1,380
	Credit	Creditors		£9,200

Circle your answer

A   B   C   D

26 In its first month of trading a business receives invoices for £12,000 worth of goods bought on credit and sells £20,000 worth of goods at list price to credit customers. The company receives 5% discount from suppliers for payment within 30 days and gives a 6% discount to its customers if they pay within 15 days.

What is the closing balance on the VAT account at the end of the month?

A   £1,110 credit
B   £1,110 debit
C   £1,200 credit
D   £1,200 debit

Circle your answer

A   B   C   D

27 The following transactions were recorded in a company's books during one week of its trading year:

	£
Trade purchases (at list price)	4,500
Sales on credit (at list price)	6,000
Purchase of a van	10,460
Entertaining	360
Purchase of a car for a sales representative	8,600

A settlement discount of £300 is available on the sales. Included in entertaining was a restaurant receipt for £180 for entertaining a M Dupont, an overseas supplier. All figures are given exclusive of VAT at 15%.

23

2: LEDGER ACCOUNTING

If the balance on the VAT account was £2,165 credit at the beginning of the week, what is the balance at the end of the week?

A £821 credit
B £776 credit
C £749 credit
D £568 debit

Circle your answer

A   B   C   D

28 A trader, registered for VAT, incurred the following transactions during the year ended 31 March 19X8:

	£
Sales taxable at standard rate	500,000
Sales taxable at zero rate	25,000
Exempt sales	75,000
Expenses subject to input tax	300,000

Included in expenses is the purchase of a motor car for £8,000 and a delivery van for £10,000.

All figures are given *exclusive* of VAT.

How much input tax can be reclaimed by the trader?

A £36,500
B £38,325
C £43,800
D £45,000

Circle your answer

A   B   C   D

CHAPTER 3

ADJUSTMENTS TO ACCOUNTS

> This chapter covers the following topics:
> - Accruals and prepayments
> - Discounts
> - Bad and doubtful debts
> - Suspense accounts

1. Accruals and prepayments

1.1 Accounts must be prepared on the basis of the accruals concept, or matching concept. This means that revenue earned in an accounting period must be matched with the expenditure incurred in earning it so as to arrive at the profit or loss for the period.

1.2 This would be a simple process if we could rely on the date of payment to indicate the date on which an expense was incurred. Unfortunately, there is often a difference between the date when an expense was incurred and the date when it was paid.

1.3 There are two main reasons for this:

- Goods and services may be provided by suppliers on credit terms. Although the benefits may be enjoyed in period 1, payment may not be due until period 2. This difficulty is dealt with by the system of debtors and creditors accounts in the nominal ledger.

- Many purchase invoices (such as an electricity bill) relate to services provided over an extended period (say three months). The expenditure must be spread over the period during which the service was enjoyed, even though payment of course takes place on a single day. This difficulty is dealt with by the system of accruals and prepayments.

1.4 An *accrual* is a liability at the year end (ie a creditor in the balance sheet). It is an expense which has not yet been entered into an expense account because no invoice has yet been received at the year end.

1.5 A *prepayment* is similar to a debtor and is a current asset in the balance sheet. It is an expense which has already been entered in an expense account (because an invoice has been received) but which is not a part of expenditure relating to the current year.

3: ADJUSTMENTS TO ACCOUNTS

1.6 It may help to clarify your ideas about this if you study the diagram below.

ACCOUNTING FOR SUPPLIERS' INVOICES

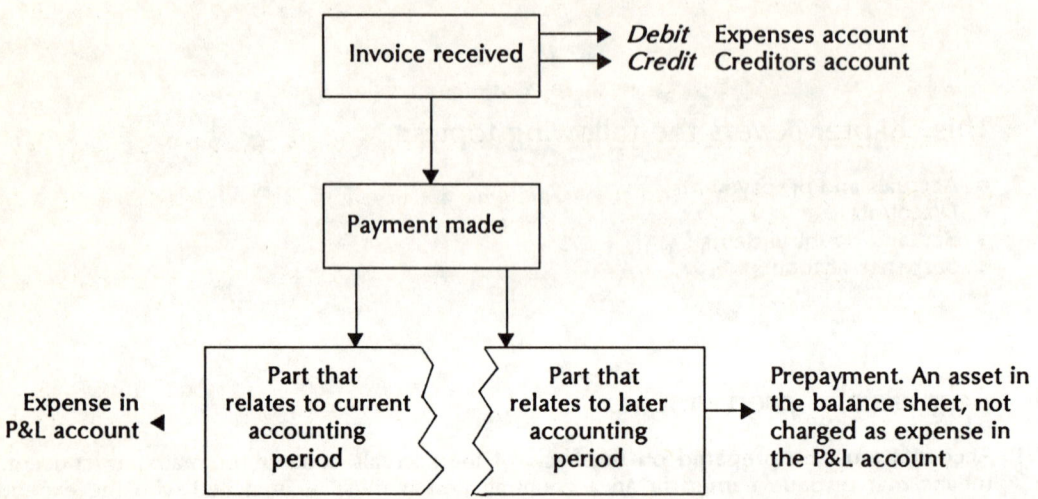

In the next period, charge the profit and loss account with the amount of the prepayment brought forward.

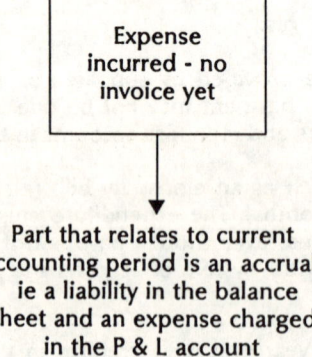

Part that relates to current accounting period is an accrual, ie a liability in the balance sheet and an expense charged in the P & L account

In the next period, when the invoice is received, post full amount of invoice to the debit of the expense account.

26

2. Discounts

2.1 A discount is a reduction in the price of goods or services. A supplier may have a *list* price at which he is prepared to provide his goods or services to the majority of customers. However, there may be reasons which justify a lower price to certain particular customers or categories of customers. In such a case, the supplier is said to allow a discount to these customers.

2.2 It is useful to distinguish between three classes of discount.

- *Trade discount* is granted to regular customers, usually those buying in bulk quantities

- *Cash discount* is granted to customers who are prepared to pay immediately in cash or by cheque, instead of purchasing on credit terms

- *Settlement discount* is granted to credit customers who pay within a specified period from the invoice date.

2.3 Cash discount and settlement discount are similar in nature. The object of both is to improve the supplier's cash flow by encouraging prompt payment. The cost of the discount to the supplier is in the nature of a financing charge, and this should be shown as an expense in the *profit and loss account*.

2.4 Trade discount is essentially different in nature. It is genuinely a reduction in the selling price made in order to attract a higher level of business. For this reason, it is accounted for as a reduction in the value of sales turnover shown in the *trading account*.

2.5 The treatment of discount on sales invoices reflects this distinction. Invoices will show the selling price of goods *after* deduction of trade discount but *before* deduction of cash or settlement discount. The price shown on the invoice will be debited to the debtor's account and credited to sales.

2.6 Cash/settlement discounts will not be reflected on invoices. If customers take advantage of them, the double entry in the supplier's books is: debit discounts allowed (an expense account in the profit and loss account), credit debtors.

2.7 The accounts of the customer mirror those of the supplier. The amounts debited to purchases and credited to creditors will be the amounts appearing on the supplier's invoices (ie they will be net of trade discounts). Settlement discounts will be a credit in the profit and loss account.

3. Bad and doubtful debts

3.1 For one reason or another, a credit customer may fail to pay his debt. When a business realises that a debtor has defaulted, it makes sense to remove the debt from the books and recognise the loss that has been suffered. The double entry is: debit bad and doubtful debts (an expense account in the profit and loss account), credit debtors (removing the debt from the ledger).

3: ADJUSTMENTS TO ACCOUNTS

3.2 Even if a customer has not yet defaulted, a business may have reason to suspect that he *will* do so. And even in cases where there is no specific suspicion, a business may know from experience that a certain proportion of its debts will never be collected. To cater for this situation, businesses may open an account called "Provision for doubtful debts".

3.3 Providing for a debt that is doubtful is different from writing off a debt that is definitely bad. A debt that is merely doubtful should not be written out of the debtors ledger; in other words, do not make the entry "credit debtors". The correct double entry is: debit bad and doubtful debts, credit provision for doubtful debts. The eventual balance on this provision account is shown as a deduction from debtors in the balance sheet.

3.4 At the end of an accounting period, management will review the level of the doubtful debts provision and decide on the level of provision required. To adjust the existing level, just make an appropriate debit or credit entry in the provision account. The double entry is completed by a credit or debit entry in the bad and doubtful debts account.

4. Suspense accounts

4.1 There are two fairly common reasons for opening a suspense account.

- Money may be received by a business for a reason which is not immediately clear to the bookkeeper. In such a case he would debit the amount to cash/bank, and would make the credit entry in a temporary suspense account. (Less commonly, the bookkeeper might be unclear about the nature of a cash *payment* made by the business.)

- A bookkeeping error might occur, so that the total debits in the nominal ledger do not equal the total credits. This might be discovered at the time of drawing up a trial balance. The solution would again be to open up a suspense account and insert the balance necessary to restore equality.

4.2 A suspense account is a temporary account. Eventually, the business must establish the nature of the suspense balance and make the entries necessary to clear it.

3: ADJUSTMENTS TO ACCOUNTS

QUESTIONS

1 Mr Bod has paid rent of £2,400 for the period 1 January 19X8 to 31 December 19X8. His first accounts are drawn up for the nine months ended 30 September 19X8.

His first accounts should show:

A only a rent expense of £2,400

B a rent expense of £1,800 and a prepayment of £600

C a rent expense of £1,800 and accrued income of £600

D a rent expense of £2,400, with an explanatory note that this is the usual charge for twelve months

Circle your answer

A   B   C   D

2 At 1 January 19X8 the accounts of a trader show accrued rent payable of £250. During the year he pays rent bills totalling £1,275, including one bill for £375 in respect of the quarter ending 31 January 19X9.

What is the profit and loss charge for rent payable for the year ended 31 December 19X8?

A £900
B £1,150
C £1,400
D £1,650

Circle your answer

A   B   C   D

Data for questions 3 - 8

A company has made the following payments in respect of rent and telephone expenses:

	Date paid	Amount £
Rent (payable quarterly in advance)		
Quarter ended 31 January 19X5	2.1.X5	480
Quarter ended 30 April 19X5	28.1.X5	480
Quarter ended 31 July 19X5	31.4.X5	810
Quarter ended 31 October 19X5	30.7.X5	810
Quarter ended 31 January 19X6	1.11.X5	810

Cont...

29

3: ADJUSTMENTS TO ACCOUNTS

	Date paid	Amount £
Telephone (payable quarterly in arrears)		
Quarter ended 30 November 19X4	1.2.X5	630
Quarter ended 28 February 19X5	1.4.X5	570
Quarter ended 31 May 19X5	17.7.X5	710
Quarter ended 31 August 19X5	12.10.X5	650
Quarter ended 30 November 19X5	1.2.X6	840
Quarter ended 28 February 19X6	2.4.X6	720

The company maintains a full double entry accounting system and has a calendar year end. All invoices for rent and telephone expenses were received on the due dates.

3 What balance should have been brought forward on the rent account at 1 January 19X5?

- A £160 debit
- B £160 credit
- C £320 debit
- D £320 credit

Circle your answer

A   B   C   D

4 What balance should have been brought forward on the telephone expenses account at 1 January 19X5?

- A £190 credit
- B £380 credit
- C £570 credit
- D £820 credit

Circle your answer

A   B   C   D

5 What balance should be carried forward on the rent payable account at 31 December 19X5?

- A £270 debit
- B £270 credit
- C £540 debit
- D £540 credit

Circle your answer

A   B   C   D

3: ADJUSTMENTS TO ACCOUNTS

6 What balance should be carried forward on the telephone expenses account at 31 December 19X5?

- A £240 credit
- B £480 credit
- C £720 credit
- D £1,080 credit

Circle your answer

A B C D

7 What will be the charge for rent payable in the profit and loss account for the year ended 31 December 19X5?

- A £2,530
- B £2,690
- C £2,800
- D £2,960

Circle your answer

A B C D

8 What will be the charge for telephone expenses in the profit and loss account for the year ended 31 December 19X5?

- A £2,820
- B £3,450
- C £4,380
- D £5,010

Circle your answer

A B C D

9 An electricity accrual of £375 was treated as a prepayment in preparing a trader's profit and loss account. As a result his profit was:

- A overstated by £375
- B understated by £375
- C overstated by £750
- D understated by £750

Circle your answer

A B C D

10 On 1 April 19X8 a company pays £60,720 in rates for the year ending 31 March 19X9. This was an increase of 10% on the charge for the previous year. In the company's profit and loss account for the year ended 31 December 19X8 what would be the charge for rates?

- A £56,166
- B £56,580
- C £59,202
- D £59,340

Circle your answer

A B C D

31

3: ADJUSTMENTS TO ACCOUNTS

11 A sole trader makes up his accounts each year to 31 May. His rent is payable quarterly in advance on 1 January, 1 April, 1 July and 1 October. Rates are set by the local authority in respect of a year running from 1 April to 31 March. They are paid each year in two equal instalments in advance on 1 April and 1 October.

His annual rental for the calendar years 19X6 and 19X7 was £6,600 and £7,200 respectively, but on 1 January 19X8 it was increased to £7,800 per annum. Local authority rates for the last three years have been:

19X6/X7	£4,800
19X7/X8	£5,400
19X8/X9	£6,000

What is the charge for rent and rates in his profit and loss account for the year ended 31 May 19X8?

A £12,900
B £12,950
C £13,000
D £13,450

Circle your answer

A   B   C   D

12 Giveaway Ltd sells goods with a list price of £12,000 to a credit customer. The customer is entitled to a 5% trade discount and also to a further $2\frac{1}{2}$% discount on list price if payment is made within ten days of the invoice date.

What amount should be credited to the sales account in Giveaway's books?

A £11,100
B £11,400
C £11,700
D £12,000

Circle your answer

A   B   C   D

13 Payquick Ltd purchases goods with a list price of £22,000. The supplier offers a 10% trade discount. Payquick also intends to pay within 20 days so as to earn a settlement discount of 2% on list price.

What entries should be made in Payquick's books to record the purchase?

A   *Debit*   Purchases   £19,800
    Credit Creditors   £19,800

B   *Debit*   Purchases   £21,560
    Credit Creditors   £21,560

Cont. . . .

3: ADJUSTMENTS TO ACCOUNTS

```
C  Debit   Purchases          £19,800
   Credit  Discounts recv.d            £440
   Credit  Creditors                 £19,360

D  Debit   Purchases          £21,560
   Credit  Discounts recv.d          £2,200
   Credit  Creditors                £19,360
```

Circle your answer

A   B   C   D

14 The cash book of Arthur Ltd has a memorandum column recording settlement discounts allowed by suppliers. The column is totalled every week and posted to the nominal ledger.

What is the correct double entry in the nominal ledger?

A Debit cash, credit discounts received
B Debit cash, credit discounts allowed
C Debit creditors, credit discount received
D Debit discounts allowed, credit debtors

Circle your answer

A   B   C   D

15 A company receives a settlement discount of £35 from a supplier. The amount is debited to the discount received account. As a result, gross profit is:

A understated by £35
B understated by £70
C overstated by £70
D unaffected

Circle your answer

A   B   C   D

16 A company receives news that a major customer has been declared bankrupt. His debt had been provided for as doubtful earlier in the year. The entries now required are:

A Debit bad and doubtful debts, credit debtors

B Debit debtors, credit bad and doubtful debts

C Debit debtors, credit provision for doubtful debts

D Debit provision for doubtful debts, credit debtors

Circle your answer

A   B   C   D

33

3: ADJUSTMENTS TO ACCOUNTS

17 Rocky Ltd is owed £1,450 by a debtor who has just gone bankrupt. The receiver has announced that creditors will receive only 30 pence in the pound. Rocky Ltd also wishes to reduce its provision for doubtful debts by £870. The effect of all this on net profit is:

- A   an increase of £435
- B   a reduction of £145
- C   a reduction of £580
- D   a reduction of £1,885

Circle your answer

A   B   C   D

18 At 31 December 19X5 the ledger of X Ltd included a £7,540 provision for doubtful debts. During the year ended 31 December 19X6 bad debts of £1,500 were written off. Debtors balances at 31 December 19X6 total £124,600 and the company wishes to carry forward a general provision of 5%.

What is the charge for bad and doubtful debts in the 19X6 profit and loss account?

- A   £115
- B   £190
- C   £2,810
- D   £2,885

Circle your answer

A   B   C   D

19 The following extracts are taken from the trial balance of Cautious Ltd at 31 December 19X6:

Debtors	£36,800
Provision for doubtful debts	£1,460

On checking the accounts it was found that a bad debt of £570 had not been written off, a debtor whose balance of £310 had been provided for was now bankrupt, and a bad debt recovered of £240 had not yet been entered in the books.

Cautious Ltd wishes to carry forward a provision of 6% of debtors balances. What is the charge or credit to profit and loss account in respect of bad and doubtful debts?

- A   Charge of £1,354
- B   Charge of £1,044
- C   Charge of £804
- D   Credit of £384

Circle your answer

A   B   C   D

20 The balances in a company's sales ledger total £76,400. Of these, one customer has disappeared without trace owing £2,300 and another, who owes £3,600, is in liquidation. The liquidator has advised that creditors are likely to receive only 40 pence in the pound. The company wishes to make a general provision of 3% on all debtors balances not specifically provided for.

3: ADJUSTMENTS TO ACCOUNTS

The balance sheet figure for debtors (net of provision) will be:

- A £68,385
- B £69,717
- C £69,782
- D £69,825

Circle your answer

A   B   C   D

21 A trial balance fails to agree by £1,000. Which one of the following errors could by itself account for the discrepancy?

- A A £1,000 cheque received from a customer, F Bloggs, had been credited to J Bloggs' account in the purchase ledger
- B A rent payment of £500 had been debited to a fixed asset account
- C A fixed asset costing £500 had been credited to purchases account
- D A £1,000 cheque paid to a supplier had been credited to the supplier's account in the purchase ledger

Circle your answer

A   B   C   D

22 Which one of the following errors would give rise to a difference on a company's trial balance?

- A Bringing forward the opening balance on an account as £9,390 instead of £9,930
- B Undercast of the sales day book by £1,000
- C Failure to record the purchase of new plant and machinery costing £5,000
- D The posting of a payment of £2,000 directors' fees to the nominal ledger account for office salaries

Circle your answer

A   B   C   D

3: ADJUSTMENTS TO ACCOUNTS

23 The preliminary trial balance of Stone Ltd did not balance and the difference was transferred to a suspense account. Which one of the following errors could *not* have caused the discrepancy?

A An error of transposition was made in balancing the sales ledger control account in the nominal ledger

B Returns inwards had been credited to the returns outwards account

C VAT on a salesman's car had been debited to the VAT account

D The bookkeeper had omitted to include cash received from the sale of a fixed asset in the disposal account

Circle your answer

A B C D

24 A sole trader withdrew business stocks for his own use. The goods had cost £220 but no entries were made in the ledger.

As a result, gross profit is:

A understated by £220
B overstated by £220
C overstated by £440
D correctly stated

Circle your answer

A B C D

25 Blunder Ltd's trial balance did not balance and a suspense account was opened to restore equality. It was discovered that:

1 the sales returns day book had been overcast by £270

2 an invoice for £2,600 was incorrectly entered in the sales day book as £6,200

3 a cheque for £500 from a credit customer had been debited to the same individual's account in the purchase ledger.

What was the original balance on the suspense account?

A £270 credit
B £500 credit
C £1,000 credit
D £3,600 credit

Circle your answer

A B C D

3: ADJUSTMENTS TO ACCOUNTS

26 Clanger Ltd's trial balance did not balance and a suspense account was opened to restore equality. It was discovered that:

1. telephone expenses of £673 had been entered in the telephone account as £763
2. a purchase invoice of £2,340 had been entered in the purchases day book as £3,240
3. discounts received of £264 had been debited to the discounts allowed account.

What was the original balance on the suspense account?

- A £528 credit
- B £618 credit
- C £1,254 credit
- D £1,518 credit

Circle your answer

A   B   C   D

27 Flufit Ltd's trial balance at 31 December 19X9 did not balance and a suspense account was opened to restore equality. It was discovered that:

1. rates of £440 which had been prepaid at 31 December 19X8 had not been brought down on the rates account as an opening balance
2. the credit side of the wages account had been under-added by £300 before the balance on the account had been determined
3. credit purchases of £1,840 had been correctly recorded in the purchases account, but were wrongly posted to the supplier's account as £1,480.

What was the original balance on the suspense account?

- A £220 credit
- B £1,100 credit
- C £380 debit
- D £500 debit

Circle your answer

A   B   C   D

28 Mr Bodgeit's trial balance did not balance and a suspense account was opened to restore equality. The balance on the suspense account was £1,508 credit. On investigating this balance it was discovered that:

1. a fixed asset had been sold during the year. The sales proceeds had been correctly recorded in the cash book but no other entries had been made
2. a prepayment of £217 and an accrual of £475 had been correctly reflected in calculating net profit, but had not been brought down as closing balances on the trial balance
3. Bodgeit is in the habit of taking business cash for his personal use. During the year this has amounted to £500. The bookkeeper has under-recorded cash sales by £500 to compensate for this, in an attempt to make the books balance.

3: ADJUSTMENTS TO ACCOUNTS

What was the amount of sales proceeds on disposal of the fixed assets?

A £750
B £1,250
C £1,750
D £1,766

Circle your answer

A   B   C   D

CHAPTER 4

FIXED ASSETS AND DEPRECIATION

> This chapter covers the following topics:
> - Depreciation of fixed assets
> - Revaluation of fixed assets
> - Disposal of fixed assets
> - Ledger accounting for fixed assets

1. Depreciation of fixed assets

1.1 The cost of purchasing a fixed asset usually consists of a single, large, payment. But the benefit of the asset may be felt over a number of accounting periods, and not just the one in which it was acquired. Depreciation is a process of spreading the original cost of a fixed asset over the accounting periods in which its benefit will be felt.

1.2 Depreciation is usually charged annually and appears as an expense in the profit and loss account. The annual charges are also accumulated in a provision account. The credit balance on this account reflects the amount of the asset's original cost which has so far been written off.

1.3 In the balance sheet, the accumulated depreciation on a fixed asset is deducted from its cost. The figure remaining is called the net book value (NBV) of the asset and represents the amount of its original cost which has not yet been written off.

1.4 The annual depreciation charge on a fixed asset is based on two factors:

- the *depreciable amount* of the asset. This is the amount which must be written off over the entire life of the asset. It consists of the original cost less any estimated residual value

- the *estimated useful life* of the asset. This may be measured in terms of years or in terms of units of service provided by the asset.

1.5 The most common methods of depreciation are:

- the *straight line method*. The depreciable amount is divided by the number of years of the asset's estimated useful life. The depreciation charge on an asset is the same each year

4: FIXED ASSETS AND DEPRECIATION

- the *reducing balance method*. A constant proportion (say 25%) of the asset's net book value is written off each year. Because the net book value is continually falling, the depreciation charge becomes less each year

- the *units of service method* (of which one example is the *machine hour method*). The depreciable amount is divided by the number of units of service (eg machine hours) expected over the asset's life. The charge each year will vary depending on the number of units of service arising in the year.

2. Revaluation of fixed assets

2.1 The net book value of a fixed asset is not intended to measure its market value. It merely represents the amount of original cost not so far written off. A business which wants to reflect the market value of its assets is at liberty to *revalue* them. This is quite commonly done in the case of assets which appreciate in value over time, especially freehold property.

2.2 When an asset is revalued, the double entry is completed through a revaluation account. It is usual to eliminate the depreciation so far accumulated by calculating the revaluation surplus as the difference between revalued amount and net book value. The revalued amount must then be depreciated over the asset's estimated remaining useful life.

3. Disposal of fixed assets

3.1 Fixed assets are not purchased by a business with the intention of re-selling them in the normal course of trade. However, the business will naturally dispose of them when their useful life is over, and may do so before then.

3.2 When an asset is disposed of there will be a profit or loss on disposal. This is calculated by comparing the disposal proceeds received by the business with the net book value of the asset.

- If disposal proceeds are *greater* than net book value a *profit* on disposal is made
- If disposal proceeds are *less* than net book value a *loss* on disposal is made.

4. Ledger accounting for fixed assets

4.1 The *purchase* of fixed assets is recorded by the double entry: debit asset account, credit bank (or creditors)

4.2 The *annual depreciation charge* is recorded by the double entry: debit depreciation expense, credit provision for accumulated depreciation.

4.3 The *revaluation* of a fixed asset is best accounted for by first stating the asset at net book value and then comparing net book value with revalued amount.

- *Stage 1*   Debit provision for accumulated depreciation
  Credit asset account
  The depreciation provision is now eliminated and the asset is stated in the asset account at NBV

- *Stage 2*   Debit asset account
  Credit revaluation reserve with the difference between revalued amount and NBV

4.4 The *disposal* of a fixed asset is accounted for by gathering together the balances relating to the asset into a single disposals account.

- *Stage 1*   Transfer the cost of the asset from the asset account: debit disposals account, credit asset account

- *Stage 2*   Transfer the accumulated depreciation from the provision account: debit provision for accumulated depreciation, credit disposals account. The balance on the disposals account is now equal to the net book value of the asset

- *Stage 3*   Record the disposal proceeds: debit bank (or debtors), credit disposals account. The balance on disposals account now represents the profit or loss on disposal.

4: FIXED ASSETS AND DEPRECIATION

QUESTIONS

1 What is the purpose of charging depreciation in accounts?

    A   To allocate the cost of a fixed asset over the accounting periods expected to benefit from its use

    B   To ensure that funds are available for the eventual replacement of the asset

    C   To reduce the cost of the asset in the balance sheet to its estimated market value

    D   To comply with the prudence concept

Circle your answer

    A   B   C   D

2 The net book value of a fixed asset represents

    A   its undepreciated cost
    B   its market value on a going concern basis
    C   its realisable value in a forced sale
    D   the amount still to be written off over its remaining life

Circle your answer

    A   B   C   D

3 A company uses the units of service method to depreciate its delivery vans. The formula for the annual depreciation charge on such a van will be

    A $\dfrac{\text{Original cost} \times \text{mileage in year}}{\text{Expected mileage over life of asset}}$

    B $\dfrac{(\text{Original cost less residual value}) \times \text{expected mileage over life of asset}}{\text{Mileage in year}}$

    C $\dfrac{\text{Depreciable amount} \times \text{mileage in year}}{\text{Expected mileage over life of asset}}$

    D $\dfrac{(\text{Depreciable amount less residual value}) \times \text{mileage in year}}{\text{Expected mileage over life of asset}}$

Circle your answer

    A   B   C   D

4: FIXED ASSETS AND DEPRECIATION

Data for questions 4 - 6

An asset costs £15,000. It has an estimated useful life of five years, after which its residual value will be £1,000.

4 If the straight line method of depreciation is used, what is the asset's net book value after one year?

- A £12,000
- B £12,200
- C £13,000
- D £13,200

Circle your answer

A B C D

5 If the reducing balance method is used, at the rate of 40% per annum, what is the asset's net book value after one year?

- A £5,600
- B £6,000
- C £8,400
- D £9,000

Circle your answer

A B C D

6 If the reducing balance method is used at 40% pa, what is the profit and loss charge for depreciation in the second year?

- A £2,400
- B £3,600
- C £5,600
- D £6,000

Circle your answer

A B C D

7 Zebedee purchases a machine for £14,000. After incurring transportation costs of £1,100 and spending £1,500 on installing the machine he is disappointed when it breaks down during the first month of operation. It costs £1,000 to repair. Zebedee depreciates his machines at the rate of 10% per annum on cost.

What is the asset's net book value after one year?

- A £12,600
- B £13,950
- C £14,940
- D £15,840

Circle your answer

A B C D

4: FIXED ASSETS AND DEPRECIATION

8 Anna Ltd purchased a delivery van on 1 January 19X6 for £12,000. Estimated mileage for the van is as follows.

Year	No of miles
19X6	15,000
19X7	21,000
19X8	19,000
19X9	20,000

At the end of 19X9, Anna Ltd expects to sell the van for about £2,000.

Using the units of service method, what will be the charge for depreciation in 19X7?

A £2,000
B £2,400
C £2,800
D £3,360

Circle your answer

A B C D

9 Brian Ltd owns freehold property which cost £78,000 to acquire (being £23,000 for the land and £55,000 for the buildings). The company's accounting policy is to depreciate buildings (but not freehold land) at the rate of 2% per annum.

After three years, what will be the net book value of the asset "freehold land and buildings" in the company's books?

A £51,700
B £73,320
C £74,700
D £76,620

Circle your answer

A B C D

10 Automat Ltd purchases a machine for which the supplier's list price is £18,000. Automat pays £13,000 in cash and trades in an old machine which has a net book value of £8,000. It is the company's policy to depreciate such machines at the rate of 10% per annum on cost.

What is the net book value of the machine after one year?

A £11,700
B £16,200
C £18,900
D £19,200

Circle your answer

A B C D

11 Limo Ltd purchases a company car for £22,000 plus VAT at 15%. The car is expected to have a life of three years and a residual value of £10,000. Payment is made partly in cash and partly by trading in an old car with a net book value of £7,800 and a trade-in value of £6,000. The company uses the straight line basis to depreciate its cars.

What is the net book value of the car after one year?

4: FIXED ASSETS AND DEPRECIATION

A £15,200
B £16,200
C £18,000
D £20,200

Circle your answer

A   B   C   D

12 A company uses the reducing balance method to depreciate its fixed assets. The annual rate is 20%. After three years the proportion of original cost still undepreciated will be:

A 51.2%
B 48.8%
C 40.0%
D impossible to determine. It depends on the estimated residual value

Circle your answer

A   B   C   D

Data for questions 13 and 14

A company purchases a machine costing £24,000. It has an expected life of five years and an expected residual value of £5,000. The company uses the straight line method of depreciation.

At the beginning of year 3, the company spends £8,000 on major technical improvements to the machine. This has the effect of extending its useful life by three years, with an expected residual value of £2,300 at the end of year 8.

13 What is the depreciable amount of the asset after the technical improvements have been made?

A £16,700
B £18,300
C £20,100
D £22,100

Circle your answer

A   B   C   D

14 What is the amount of the depreciation charge in year 4?

A £2,762
B £3,683
C £3,712
D £4,950

Circle your answer

A   B   C   D

45

4: FIXED ASSETS AND DEPRECIATION

15 At the end of an accounting period a company calculates the amount of depreciation to be charged on its fixed assets. What double entry is required to record this transaction?

A Debit provision for depreciation, credit depreciation expense

B Debit fixed assets, credit depreciation expense

C Debit depreciation expense, credit fixed assets

D Debit depreciation expense, credit provision for depreciation

Circle your answer

A   B   C   D

Data for questions 16 and 17

Small Carriers Ltd operates a haulage contracting business. At 1 April 19X7 the following balances appeared in the books:

	£
Motor vans (at cost)	37,300
Motor vans provision for depreciation	14,700

On 30 September 19X7 one of the old vans, which originally cost £12,000 on 1 August 19X5, was accepted in part exchange for a new van costing £14,000. The balance of cost on the new van was settled by a cheque for £8,500.

The company's depreciation policy is 20% per annum on the cost of vans, with a full year's charge in the year of acquisition and no charge in the year of disposal.

16 What is the balance sheet figure for *cost* of motor vans at 31 March 19X8?

A   £33,800
B   £35,300
C   £39,300
D   £41,000

Circle your answer

A   B   C   D

4: FIXED ASSETS AND DEPRECIATION

17 What is the balance sheet figure for *accumulated depreciation* on motor vans at 31 March 19X8?

A £15,360
B £17,360
C £17,760
D £22,560

Circle your answer

A   B   C   D

18 A company buys a machine on 31 August 19X3 for £44,000. It has an expected life of seven years and an estimated residual value of £2,000. On 30 June 19X7 the machine is disposed of for £18,000. The company's year end is 31 December. Its accounting policy is to charge depreciation using the straight line method with a proportionate charge in the years of acquisition and disposal.

Calculate the profit or loss on disposal of the machine.

A Loss of £3,500
B Loss of £3,000
C Loss of £2,000
D Profit of £4,000

Circle your answer

A   B   C   D

19 A company wishes to purchase a motor car with a list price of £12,200. The dealer agrees to accept £7,500 cash together with a part exchange on an old car belonging to the company. The part exchange car originally cost £10,300 and has a net book value of £4,300.

How should the trade-in value be reflected in the company's ledger?

A *Debit*   Motor car a/c   £4,700
   Credit Motor cars dis-
             posal a/c   £4,700

B *Debit*   Cash   £4,700
   Credit Motor cars dis-
             posal a/c   £4,700

C *Debit*   Motor cars dis-
             posal a/c   £4,300
   Credit Motor cars a/c   £4,300

D *Debit*   Motor cars a/c   £4,300
   Credit Motor cars dis-
             posal a/c   £4,300

Circle your answer

A   B   C   D

4: FIXED ASSETS AND DEPRECIATION

20 A business purchased a fixed asset on credit at a cost of £70,000. It used its own work force to install the asset, and the labour cost of this work was £7,000.
The entries needed to record all this are:

A	*Debit*	Asset account	£70,000	
	Credit	Bank		£70,000
B	*Debit*	Asset account	£77,000	
	Credit	Bank		£77,000
C	*Debit*	Asset account	£70,000	
	Debit	Wages account	£7,000	
	Credit	Bank		£77,000
D	*Debit*	Asset account	£77,000	
	Credit	Creditors		£70,000
	Credit	Bank		£7,000

Circle your answer

A   B   C   D

21 A ledger account for "plant and machinery at cost" includes a debit entry of £4,000 with the narrative "plant disposals account".

This entry indicates:

A   that the business has disposed of an asset which originally cost £4,000

B   that the business has disposed of an asset with a net book value of £4,000

C   that the business has disposed of an asset with a trade-in value of £4,000

D   that the business has acquired an asset costing £4,000

Circle your answer

A   B   C   D

CHAPTER 5

ACCOUNTING FOR STOCKS

> This chapter covers the following topics:
> - Establishing quantities of stocks
> - The principles of stock valuation
> - Methods of attributing costs to units of stock

1. Establishing quantities of stocks

1.1 The quantities of stock held by a business are usually established by means of a physical count. Stock movements should be kept to a minimum during the period of the count and should be recorded very carefully to avoid double-counting or omission of stock items. Ideally, the count should take place while the business is closed down (eg at a weekend).

1.2 Some companies maintain a system of continuous stock records, often on computers. This enables a stock figure to be produced at any time that it is needed. Even with this system, however, periodic stocktakes will be necessary as a check on the accuracy of the records.

1.3 Two particular points are worth mentioning in connection with stocktaking.

- A company may receive free samples from potential suppliers. These should not be regarded as trading stocks. They should be excluded from the stock count and the stock valuation.

- A company may send 'sale or return' goods to customers. The customers have the option to return the goods if they are unable to sell them on. Until the customer confirms that he has been able to sell the goods, the company cannot take credit for any sale. But because the company has not sold the goods, it follows that they still form part of stock in hand, even though they are not on the company's own premises.

2. The principles of stock valuation

2.1 The need to value closing stocks arises from the accruals concept. The cost of purchasing such stocks arises in period 1, but will not produce revenue until the goods are sold in period 2. As a result, the cost must be carried forward and charged against profits in the later period.

5: ACCOUNTING FOR STOCKS

2.2 The amount carried forward in this way would normally be the *cost* of the stocks. But there are circumstances in which net realisable value (NRV) will be lower than cost, and in such cases prudence dictates that the lower valuation should be used. This argument leads to the general rule for valuation of stock in the balance sheet.

> Stock is stated at the lower of cost and NRV

2.3 In theory, the comparison of cost and net realisable value should be carried out separately for each individual item of stock. In practice, this might be very time consuming and it could be preferable to group units of stock into categories before carrying out the comparison.

2.4 All of this assumes that we know the cost and the NRV of each stock item (or each stock category).

- Calculate NRV by taking the estimated selling price of the stock item and then deducting any costs that are still to be incurred on it. These might include manufacturing costs to complete the product, and also costs of storing, distributing and selling the product.

- Cost includes the price of any raw materials or components purchased from outside suppliers. But it also includes any costs (such as labour costs) incurred in converting such raw materials into work in progress or finished goods.

3. Methods of attributing costs to units of stock

3.1 Businesses may purchase particular stock items frequently. When the stock is stored, different consignments will mingle together. If the various consignments have been purchased at different unit prices, it becomes a problem to allocate a purchase price to units issued to production and units still in stock at the period end.

3.2 Several techniques are used in practice.

- FIFO (first in, first out). Using this technique, we assume that components are used in the order in which they are received from suppliers. The components issued to production are deemed to have formed part of the oldest consignment still unused and are costed accordingly.

- LIFO (last in, first out). This involves the opposite assumption, that components issued to production originally formed part of the most recent delivery, while older consignments lie in the bin undisturbed.

- Average cost. As purchase prices change with each new consignment, the average price of components in the bin is constantly changed. Each component in the bin at any moment is assumed to have been purchased at the average price of all components in the bin at that moment.

5: ACCOUNTING FOR STOCKS

- Standard cost. A pre-determined standard cost is applied to all stock items. If this standard price differs from prices actually paid during the period it will be necessary to write off the difference as a variance in the profit and loss account.

- Replacement cost. The arbitrary assumption is made that the cost at which a stock unit was purchased is the amount it would cost to replace it. This is often (but not necessarily) the unit cost of stocks purchased in the next consignment *following* the issue of the component to production. For this reason, a method which produces similar results to replacement costs is called NIFO (next in, first out).

5: ACCOUNTING FOR STOCKS

QUESTIONS

1 Justin Ltd's stock valuation excludes goods held by customers on a sale or return basis. The goods have a cost to the company of £1,200 and a selling price to customers of £1,700. They have not been invoiced to customers.

The effect on Justin Ltd's profit of excluding this stock is that:

A profit is understated by £500
B profit is understated by £1,200
C profit is understated by £1,700
D profit is stated correctly

Circle your answer

A B C D

2 Justin Ltd's stock valuation also excludes a number of free samples from potential suppliers. They would normally cost £300 and could probably be sold to Justin Ltd's customers for £550.

The effect on the company's profit of excluding this stock is that:

A profit is understated by £250
B profit is understated by £300
C profit is understated by £550
D profit is stated correctly

Circle your answer

A B C D

3 Jeremy Ltd's stock valuation excludes goods supplied to a customer on a sale or return basis. Jeremy Ltd purchased the goods for £7,200 and invoiced them at a mark-up of 40% on selling price.

The effect on Jeremy Ltd's profit of this accounting treatment is that:

A profit is overstated by £2,880
B profit is overstated by £4,800
C profit is overstated by £7,200
D profit is stated correctly

Circle your answer

A B C D

4 Jemima's stock valuation includes certain damaged goods at their original cost of £2,655. These could be repaired at a cost of £420 and sold for £2,900.

The effect on Jemima's profit of including these goods at cost is that:

A profit is overstated by £175
B profit is overstated by £2,655
C profit is understated by £2,480
D profit is stated correctly

Circle your answer

A B C D

5: ACCOUNTING FOR STOCKS

5 John Ltd's stock valuation includes goods received from Jeremy Ltd on a sale or return basis. The goods have been invoiced by Jeremy Ltd at £12,000 and John Ltd would expect to sell them to customers for £16,000. John Ltd has not recorded the purchase invoice in its books.

The effect on John Ltd's profit of including these goods in the stock valuation at their cost of £12,000 is that:

A   profit is overstated by £12,000
B   profit is understated by £4,000
C   profit is understated by £12,000
D   profit is stated correctly

Circle your answer

A   B   C   D

6 Jingle purchases goods with a list price of £8,000. The supplier grants a trade discount of 5% on list price, and Jingle also takes advantage of a settlement discount amounting to 2% of list price.

In Jingle's balance sheet the value of this stock should be:

A   £7,200
B   £7,600
C   £7,840
D   £8,000

Circle your answer

A   B   C   D

7 Junket Ltd's year end is 31 December. For various reasons, stock could not be counted this year until 6 January. The stock valuation at this date was £74,300. Detailed records were kept of stock movements between the year end and the stocktake. The following figures (all stated at cost) are available:

	£
Sales	1,250
Purchases	1,155
Returns inwards	275
Returns outwards	140

The value of stock in Junket Ltd's balance sheet at 31 December is:

A   £74,070
B   £74,260
C   £74,340
D   £74,530

Circle your answer

A   B   C   D

5: ACCOUNTING FOR STOCKS

8 Jamboree's draft balance sheet includes a stock figure of £25,850. On further investigation, the following facts are discovered:

1. One stock sheet had been over-added by £212 and another under-added by £74.

2. Goods included at their cost of £460 had deteriorated. They could still be sold at their normal selling price (£800) once repair work costing £270 was complete

3. Goods costing £430 sent to customers on a sale or return basis had been included in stock at their selling price of £665.

The corrected figure for stock in Jamboree's balance sheet is:

A £25,047
B £25,477
C £25,547
D £25,753

Circle your answer

A   B   C   D

9 The stock of Jordan Ltd includes the following three items

	Supplier's list price £	Net realisable value £
Product A	240	272
Product B	281	385
Product C	172	157
	693	814

At what total value should these items be stated in the balance sheet of Jordan Ltd?

A £678
B £693
C £814
D £829

Circle your answer

A   B   C   D

10 Jordan Ltd's stock also includes three items for which the following details are available

	Supplier's list price £	Net realisable value £
Product D	3,600	5,100
Product E	2,900	2,800
Product F	4,200	4,100
	10,700	12,000

5: ACCOUNTING FOR STOCKS

The company receives a 2½% trade discount from its suppliers, and also takes advantage of a 2% discount for prompt payment.

At what total value should products D, E and F be stated in the balance sheet of Jordan Ltd?

A £10,219
B £10,405
C £10,428
D £10,433

Circle your answer

A   B   C   D

11 The following information relates to Jonathan Ltd's year-end stock of finished goods.

	Direct costs of materials and labour	Production overheads incurred	Expected selling and distribution overheads	Expected selling price
	£	£	£	£
Stock category 1	2,470	2,100	480	5,800
Stock category 2	9,360	2,730	150	12,040
Stock category 3	1,450	850	290	2,560
	13,280	5,680	920	20,400

At what amount should finished goods stock be stated in the company's balance sheet?

A £13,280
B £18,730
C £18,960
D £19,650

Circle your answer

A   B   C   D

12 Jehu's accounts showed a gross profit for the year of £27,200. After the accounts were prepared it was found that the opening stock had been overstated by £1,200 while closing stock had been understated by £1,700.

What is the amount of Jehu's corrected gross profit for the year?

A £24,300
B £26,700
C £27,700
D £30,100

Circle your answer

A   B   C   D

55

5: ACCOUNTING FOR STOCKS

13 The following details are taken from the books of Jumbo Ltd:

	£		£
Opening stock	2,850	Purchases	37,640
Closing stock	4,270	Returns inwards	2,770
Carriage outwards	3,110	Carriage inwards	1,840

What is the company's cost of goods sold?

A £35,290
B £38,060
C £39,480
D £41,170

Circle your answer

A   B   C   D

14 Jenkins Ltd has 200 identical units of stock. Each one cost £60 originally and they would be ready for sale after modification work costing £12 per unit. Their selling price would then be £100 each, but the company would incur selling costs of 8% of sales value.

Calculate the total balance sheet value of this stock.

A £12,000
B £14,400
C £16,000
D £18,400

Circle your answer

A   B   C   D

15 James Ltd purchased raw materials for £4,720 and paid £125 transporting the materials to its own premises. Conversion costs incurred amounted to £2,115 by 31 December 19X8. At that date, costs of £845 were still required to get the goods into a saleable condition. The estimated eventual selling price is £8,200; selling and distribution costs will amount to 4% of selling price.

At what value should this work in progress be stated in the balance sheet of James Ltd at 31 December 19X8?

A £4,845
B £6,960
C £7,027
D £7,872

Circle your answer

A   B   C   D

5: ACCOUNTING FOR STOCKS

Data for questions 16 - 18

John makes purchases as follows in his first period of trading:

	Units	Price per unit £
3 January 19X8	15	26
18 February 19X8	35	28
11 March 19X8	28	23
20 April 19X8	45	32
12 May 19X8	10	33
20 June 19X8	8	35

On 27 June John sells 100 units for £40 each.

16 In his balance sheet at 30 June 19X8 what is the value of John's stock, assuming he uses the FIFO basis?

A £1,118
B £1,182
C £1,346
D £1,640

Circle your answer

A   B   C   D

17 In his balance sheet at 30 June 19X8 what is the value of John's stock assuming he uses the LIFO basis?

A £1,118
B £1,182
C £1,346
D £1,640

Circle your answer

A   B   C   D

18 In his balance sheet at 30 June 19X8 what is the value of John's stock assuming he uses the average cost basis?

A £1,118
B £1,182
C £1,346
D £1,640

Circle your answer

A   B   C   D

5: ACCOUNTING FOR STOCKS

Data for questions 19 - 21

Jones, a sole trader, had 3,000 components in stock at 1 January with a value of £1.74 each. During January and February the following stock movements occurred.

Date	Receipts Quantity	Unit price	Issues Quantity	Unit price
5 January	20,000	£1.68		
15 January			16,000	£1.68
20 January	24,000	£1.72		
8 February	26,000	£1.75		
10 February			24,000	£1.75
12 February			4,000	£1.735
25 February	20,000	£1.78		
27 February			40,000	£1.75

19 What method is Jones using to charge issues to production?

A LIFO
B FIFO
C Replacement cost
D Average cost

Circle your answer

A   B   C   D

20 How many components remain in stock at the end of February?

A 69,000
B 49,000
C 9,000
D 6,000

Circle your answer

A   B   C   D

21 What value will Jones place on his stock at the end of February?

A £10,160
B £15,300
C £15,380
D £15,600

Circle your answer

A   B   C   D

5: ACCOUNTING FOR STOCKS

22 Jock is a manufacturer of stationery. During his stocktake he discovered that a quantity of stationery of a large standard size had been damaged. The damage was confined to the edges of the paper and it would be possible to reduce the stock to a smaller standard size by guillotining the damaged portion.

The production cost of this quantity of large paper was £17,000 and it would normally sell for £28,000. The same number of sheets of the smaller paper would normally cost £12,000 to produce and they would sell for £18,000.

The company's selling and distribution costs are calculated as 5% of selling price. The estimated costs of reducing the damaged paper to the smaller size are £500.

Calculate the balance sheet value of this stock item.

A £12,000
B £16,600
C £17,000
D £17,500

Circle your answer

A   B   C   D

23 In a period of rapid inflation which of the following methods of charging stock issues to production will give the lowest gross profit figure?

A Average cost
B LIFO
C FIFO
D Replacement cost

Circle your answer

A   B   C   D

24 Goods sent to a customer on a sale or return basis are to be included in stock at the year end. The following details are available:

	£
Cost of purchase	1,000
Cost of conversion	500
Carriage outwards	150
Selling costs	200
Selling price	2,000

At what value should the stocks be recorded in the balance sheet?

A £1,500
B £1,650
C £1,800
D £1,850

Circle your answer

A   B   C   D

CHAPTER 6

CONTROL ACCOUNTS AND BANK RECONCILIATIONS

> This chapter covers the following topics:
>
> - Control accounts for debtors and creditors
> - Control accounts for wages and salaries
> - Bank reconciliations

1. Control accounts for debtors and creditors

1.1 A control account is a *total* account. Its balance represents an asset or a liability which is the grand total of many individual assets or liabilities. These individual assets/liabilities must be separately detailed in subsidiary accounting records, but their total is conveniently available in the control account ready for immediate use.

1.2 Most businesses operate control accounts for trade debtors and creditors, but such accounts may be useful in other areas too. In particular, the use of VAT control accounts has already featured in chapter 2, while control accounts for wages and salaries are covered later in this chapter.

1.3 The double entry relating to debtors and creditors can be confusing. The key is to realise that the accounts of individuals are maintained *for memorandum purposes only*. This means that entering a sales invoice, say, in the account of an individual debtor is not part of the double entry process.

1.4 So how *are* sales invoices introduced into the double entry system? The answer is illustrated in the diagram overleaf. The invoices in the sales day book are totalled periodically and the total amount is posted as follows:

Debit Debtors control account
Credit Sales account.

Similarly, the *total* of cash receipts from debtors is posted from the cash book to the credit of the debtors control account.

6: CONTROL ACCOUNTS AND BANK RECONCILIATIONS

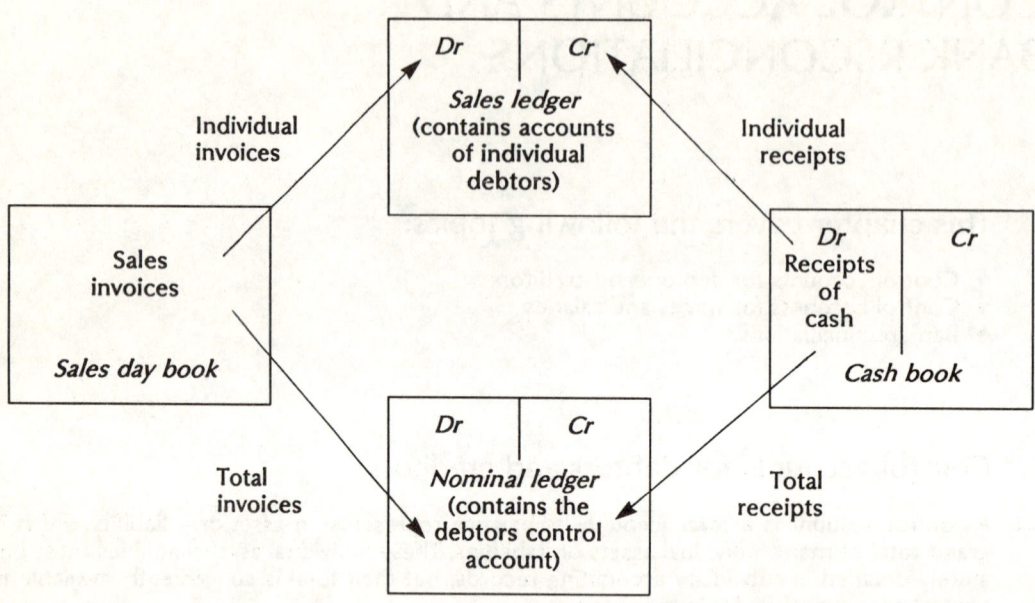

Accounting for credit sales

1.5 In the same way, the creditors control account is credited with the total purchase invoices logged in the purchase day book, and debited with the total of cash payments to suppliers.

1.6 It is worth bearing in mind the main reasons for maintaining both individual accounts and a control account.

- The individual accounts are necessary for administrative convenience. For example, a customer may wish to query the balance owed by himself to the business; to deal with his query, sales ledger staff would refer to his individual account.

- The control accounts provide a convenient total which can be used immediately in extracting a trial balance or preparing accounts. Their pure control function is also important: a reconciliation between the control account total and the sales ledger will help to detect errors.

2. Control accounts for wages and salaries

2.1 There are various ways of accounting for wages and salaries but the most common method involves the use of three control accounts:

Wages and salaries control account
PAYE control account
NIC control account

2.2 The first step is to calculate the total costs of employment to be borne by the business. These consist of employees' gross pay plus employer's National Insurance contributions. The double entry is then:

Debit Wages and salaries expense account (P&L account)
Credit Wages and salaries control account (gross pay)
Credit NIC control account (employer's NIC).

2.3 The amount of deductions must be calculated for PAYE and employees' NIC. These amounts are debited to wages and salaries control account and credited to PAYE control account and NIC control account respectively.

2.4 The remaining credit balance on wages and salaries control account is then eliminated by paying employees their net pay: credit cash, debit wages and salaries control.

2.5 In due course, the credit balances on PAYE control and NIC control are eliminated by making payments to Inland Revenue.

2.6 Any voluntary deductions permitted by employees must be debited to wages and salaries control account and credited to a liability account until they are eventually paid over by the employer as appropriate.

3. Bank reconciliations

3.1 In theory, the entries appearing on a business's bank statement should be exactly the same as those in the business cash book. The balance shown by the bank statement as on a particular date should be the same as the cash book balance at the same date.

3.2 It is common (and a very important financial control) to check this at regular intervals, say weekly or monthly. Invariably it will be found that the picture shown by the bank statement differs from that shown by the cash book. The reasons for this fall into three categories:

- *errors*. Entries on the bank statement may be incorrect, but more commonly, errors may be found in the cash book;

- *omissions*. Items may appear on the bank statement which have not yet been entered in the cash book. These may include bank charges and payments made by direct debit;

- *timing differences*. Cheques are entered in the cash book as soon as they are written, but there may be a delay before the payee receives them and a further delay while they are processed through the bank clearing system.

3.3 When these discrepancies are noticed, appropriate adjustments must be made. Errors must be corrected; omissions from the cash book must be made good. The balance in the cash book will then be correct and up to date. Any remaining difference between the cash book balance and the statement balance should then be explained as the result of identifiable timing differences.

6: CONTROL ACCOUNTS AND BANK RECONCILIATIONS

QUESTIONS

1 The total of the purchase day book is posted:

A to the debit of the supplier's account
B to the debit of the purchases account
C to the credit of the customer's account
D to the credit of the purchases account

Circle your answer

A (B) C D

2 Which one of the following items would *not* appear in a debtors control account?

A Provision for doubtful debts
B Returns inwards
C Discounts allowed
D Interest charged on overdue accounts

Circle your answer

(A) B C D

3 The following information is taken from the books of a business:

	£
Debtors at 1 January 19X8	22,500
Debtors at 31 December 19X8	27,300
Credit sales in 19X8	107,800

The cash received from debtors during 19X8 amounted to:

A £80,500
B £85,300
C £103,000
D £112,600

Circle your answer

A B C D

4 A debtors control account contains the following entries:

	£
Balance brought forward at 1 January	21,400
Bank	102,000
Discounts allowed	8,125
Credit sales	120,100

64

6: CONTROL ACCOUNTS AND BANK RECONCILIATIONS

There are no other entries in the account. What is the closing balance carried forward at 31 December?

A £4,825
B £11,525
C £31,375
D £47,625

Circle your answer

A   B   C   D

5 A creditors control account contains the following entries:

	£
Bank	79,500
Credit purchases	83,200
Discounts received	3,750
Contra with debtors control account	4,000
Balance c/f at 31 December 19X8	12,920

There are no other entries in the account. What was the opening balance brought forward at 1 January 19X8?

A £8,870
B £8,970
C £16,970
D £24,370

Circle your answer

A   B   C   D

6 After you have paid a creditor £1,000 he informs you that you were entitled to a settlement discount of 5% which you forgot to deduct. What is the correct double entry to rectify this error in your books?

A *Debit* Discount allowed
   Credit Creditors account

B *Debit* Creditors account
   Credit Discount received

C *Debit* Bank account
   Credit Discount received

D *Debit* Discount received
   Credit Creditors account

Circle your answer

A   B   C   D

65

6: CONTROL ACCOUNTS AND BANK RECONCILIATIONS

7 The balance on a company's creditors control account differs from the total of creditors' balances in the purchase ledger. Which one of the following occurrences might account for the discrepancy?

- A A trade discount was calculated incorrectly
- B A cheque payment to a supplier was omitted from the books
- C The total of cash receipts in the cash book was miscast
- D Returns outwards were not entered in the personal account of a supplier

Circle your answer

A   B   C   D

8 The following information is available about a company's debtors:

	£
Balance b/f at 1 January 19X8	13,850
Provision for doubtful debts at 1 January 19X8	1,110
Increase in provision during 19X8	120
Discount allowed in year	3,940
Sales in year	121,730
Purchase ledger contras in year	8,900
Receipts from customers in year	114,200

What is the balance carried forward at 31 December 19X8 on the debtors control account?

- A £7,310
- B £8,420
- C £8,540
- D £26,340

Circle your answer

A   B   C   D

Data for questions 9 - 10

Womble & Sons have an accounting year ended 31 December 19X8. At that date the balance on the sales ledger control account was £65,000, but the total of the individual accounts in the sales ledger came to £63,620. Upon investigation the following facts were discovered.

1. The sales day book total for week 49 had been overcast by £300.
2. A credit balance of £210 on Orinocco's account in the sales ledger had been incorrectly treated as a debit entry, when balancing off his account.
3. A purchase ledger contra of £1,500 had been entered in Bungo's account in the sales ledger but no other entry had been made.

6: CONTROL ACCOUNTS AND BANK RECONCILIATIONS

9 The adjusted balance on the sales ledger control account is:

  A £62,780
  B £63,200
  C £63,620
  D £64,700

Circle your answer

A   B   C   D

10 The adjusted total of sales ledger balances is:

  A £62,780
  B £63,200
  C £63,620
  D £64,700

Circle your answer

A   B   C   D

11 The following information relates to a company's year ended 31 December 19X5:

	£
Opening balance on debtors control account	21,000
Closing balance on debtors control account	28,000
Bills of exchange accepted by customers	17,000
Sales (including VAT at 15%)	103,500

The amount of cash received from customers was:

  A £63,975
  B £66,000
  C £79,500
  D £113,500

Circle your answer

A   B   C   D

12 The total of the balances in a company's sales ledger is £800 more than the debit balance on its debtors control account. Which one of the following errors could by itself account for the discrepancy?

  A The sales day book has been undercast by £800

  B Settlement discounts totalling £800 have been omitted from the nominal ledger

  C One sales ledger account with a credit balance of £800 has been treated as a debit balance

  D The cash receipts book has been undercast by £800

Circle your answer

A   B   C   D

6: CONTROL ACCOUNTS AND BANK RECONCILIATIONS

Data for questions 13-14

The balances in a company's sales ledger at 31 December were totalled and their sum was found to be £83,795. At the same date, the debit balance on the company's debtors control account was £82,511.

Upon investigation the following facts were discovered:

1. One customer, whose balance was £420 credit, had been omitted from the list of sales ledger balances
2. A bad debt of £500 had not been entered in the nominal ledger
3. Cash received of £280 had been debited to the customer's personal account
4. A customer's cheque for £804 had been dishonoured by the bank, but no adjustment had been made in the control account

13 The adjusted total of sales ledger balances is:

A £81,207
B £82,815
C £83,655
D £83,935

Circle your answer

A B C D

14 The adjusted balance on the sales ledger control account is:

A £81,207
B £82,815
C £83,655
D £83,935

Circle your answer

A B C D

15 The total cost of wages and salaries debited in a business's profit and loss account is equal to:

A the total net pay received by all employees

B the total gross pay earned by all employees

C the total gross pay earned by all employees plus employees' NI contributions

D the total gross pay earned by all employees plus employer's NI contributions

Circle your answer

A B C D

6: CONTROL ACCOUNTS AND BANK RECONCILIATIONS

16 During the monthly payroll routine of Colossal plc it was found that employer's NI contributions amounted to £1,500,000. What entries should be made to record this sum in the company's accounts?

- A *Debit* Wages and salaries control account
     Credit Wages and salaries expense account

- B *Debit* Wages and salaries expense account
     Credit Wages and salaries control account

- C *Debit* Wages and salaries control account
     Credit NIC control account

- D *Debit* Wages and salaries expense account
     Credit NIC control account

Circle your answer

A   B   C   D

17 The employees of Openhand Ltd contribute to a local charity by means of a deduction from their monthly salary payments. What double entry is required to enter these deductions into the company's books each month?

- A *Debit* Charitable expenses account
     Credit Wages and salaries expense account

- B *Debit* Wages and salaries control account
     Credit Charitable contributions control account

- C *Debit* Charitable contributions control account
     Credit Wages and salaries control account

- D *Debit* Wages and salaries expense account
     Credit Charitable expenses account

Circle your answer

A   B   C   D

6: CONTROL ACCOUNTS AND BANK RECONCILIATIONS

18 Brian Hardup has received a loan from his employer. The loan is being repaid by means of deductions from Brian's monthly salary payments. What double entry is required to enter these repayments into the business's books each month?

A *Debit*   Loan account
   Credit Wages and salaries expense account

B *Debit*   Wages and salaries expense account
   Credit Bank

C *Debit*   Wages and salaries control account
   Credit Loan account

D *Debit*   Bank
   Credit Wages and salaries expense account

Circle your answer

A   B   C   D

Data for questions 19 - 21

The following information is available in respect of Bottomline Ltd:

	£
Balances at 1 December 19X8	
PAYE control account	22,486
NIC control account	14,731
Wages and salaries summary for December 19X8	
Total gross pay	54,410
PAYE	13,930
Employees' NIC	4,310
Employer's NIC	8,750
Employees' savings deductions	1,270
Payments to Inland Revenue during December 19X8	
In respect of PAYE	8,920
In respect of NIC	8,240

19 The total amount of net pay received by employees in December 19X8 was:

A £30,460
B £34,900
C £35,980
D £43,650

Circle your answer

A   B   C   D

6: CONTROL ACCOUNTS AND BANK RECONCILIATIONS

20 The balance on the PAYE control account at 31 December 19X8 was:

- A £13,930
- B £17,476
- C £27,496
- D £45,336

Circle your answer

A B C D

21 The balance on the NIC control account at 31 December 19X8 was:

- A £9,911
- B £10,801
- C £15,241
- D £19,551

Circle your answer

A B C D

22 A company's cash book shows a debit balance of £700. The bank statement as at the same date shows an overdrawn balance of £210. Which one of the following timing differences could account for the discrepancy?

- A Cheques drawn but not yet presented amounted to £490
- B Cheques received but not yet cleared amounted to £490
- C Cheques drawn but not yet presented amounted to £910
- D Cheques received but not yet cleared amounted to £910

Circle your answer

A B C D

23 A company's bank statement shows £715 direct debits and £353 investment income not recorded in the cash book. The bank statement does not show a customer's cheque for £875 entered in the cash book on the last day of the accounting period. If the cash book shows a credit balance of £610 what balance appears on the bank statement?

- A £97 overdrawn
- B £627 overdrawn
- C £1,123 overdrawn
- D £1,847 overdrawn

Circle your answer

A B C D

6: CONTROL ACCOUNTS AND BANK RECONCILIATIONS

24 A company's cash book at 31 December 19X8 shows a debit balance of £2,125. When the bank statement as at that date is received it is found that cheques drawn by the company totalling £274 had not been presented. In addition, the statement recorded bank charges of £58 which had not been entered in the cash book.

What was the balance on the bank statement as at 31 December 19X8?

A £1,909 overdrawn balance
B £1,909 favourable balance
C £2,341 favourable balance
D £2,457 favourable balance

Circle your answer

A   B   C   D

25 A company's bank statement shows an overdraft of £3,204 at 31 March 19X7. The statement includes bank charges of £46 which have not yet been recorded in the company's cash book. The statement does not include cheques for £780 paid to suppliers, nor an amount of £370 received from a debtor; both of these amounts appear in the bank statement for April 19X7.

If the company prepares a balance sheet at 31 March 19X7, the figure for the bank overdraft should be:

A £2,748
B £2,794
C £3,568
D £3,614

Circle your answer

A   B   C   D

26 A company's bank statement shows an overdraft of £197 at the end of month 1. The statement includes bank charges of £17 which have not yet been recorded in the company's cash book. The statement does not include a cheque for £340 paid to a supplier, nor an amount of £216 received from a debtor; both of these amounts appear in the bank statement for month 2.

If the company prepares a balance sheet as at the end of month 1, the figure for bank overdraft should be:

A £56
B £73
C £304
D £321

Circle your answer

A   B   C   D

6: CONTROL ACCOUNTS AND BANK RECONCILIATIONS

Data for questions 27 - 28

The bank statement of a business at 30 June shows a favourable balance of £167. The following additional information is available:

1. Cheques totalling £394 sent out by the company before 30 June were not cleared until July.

2. Two items on the bank statement had not been recorded in the cash book: a credit transfer of £850 from a customer and bank overdraft interest of £112.

3. Cheques from customers totalling £643 were paid into the bank on 30 June but were not cleared until July.

27 If the business prepares a balance sheet at 30 June what will be the figure for cash at bank or bank overdraft?

A £416 cash at bank
B £82 overdraft
C £322 overdraft
D £820 overdraft

Circle your answer

A B C D

28 What was the original (unadjusted) cash book balance as at 30 June?

A £322 debit
B £322 credit
C £416 debit
D £416 credit

Circle your answer

A B C D

CHAPTER 7

INCOMPLETE RECORDS

> This chapter covers the following topics:
> - Sales and debtors, purchases and creditors
> - The two-column cash book
> - Gross margins and mark-ups

1. Sales and debtors, purchases and creditors

1.1 Many small businesses do not keep a full set of accounting records, usually because they do not have staff with the necessary bookkeeping ability. Even where full records *are* maintained, there is a danger that they may be accidentally lost or destroyed. For both of these reasons, you need to be able to cope with the problems of incomplete records.

1.2 In many cases, the problems can be reduced to simple arithmetic. For example, suppose the accounting records of a business contain no more than a file of bank statements, a file of unpaid suppliers' invoices and a list of amounts owed by customers. This information should be enough to produce the trading account figures for sales and cost of sales.

1.3 The key lies in the formulae linking

- sales, cash receipts and debtors
- purchases, cash payments and creditors.

> Opening debtors + sales - cash receipts = closing debtors

> Opening creditors + purchases - cash payments = closing creditors

1.4 Opening debtors and creditors will be known from last year's balance sheet; cash movements are known from the bank statements; provided there is a record of closing debtors and creditors, the equations can be manipulated to arrive at the figures for sales and purchases.

1.5 Less commonly it may happen that one of the other figures in these equations is the unknown. Provided that there is only one missing figure, it can always be derived by simple arithmetic.

7: INCOMPLETE RECORDS

2. The two-column cash book

2.1 Incomplete records problems often concern small retail businesses where sales are mainly for cash. A two-column cash book is often the key to preparing final accounts.

- The *bank* column records cheques drawn on the business bank account and cheques received from customers and other sources.

- The *cash* column records till receipts and any expenses or drawings paid out of till receipts before banking.

Debits (receipts)		Credits (payments)	
Cash £	Bank £	Cash £	Bank £

2.2 Don't forget that movements between cash and bank need to be recorded by contra entries. This will usually be cash receipts lodged in the bank (debit bank column, credit cash column), but could also be withdrawals of cash from the bank to top up the till (debit cash column, credit bank column).

2.3 Again, incomplete records problems will often feature an unknown figure to be derived. Enter in the credit of the cash book column all amounts known to have been paid from till receipts: expenses, drawings, lodgements into bank. Enter in the debit of the cash book column all receipts from cash customers or other cash sources.

- The balancing figure may then be a large debit, representing the value of cash sales if that is the unknown figure.

- Alternatively it may be a credit entry that is needed to balance, representing the amount of cash drawings or of cash stolen.

3. Gross margins and mark-ups

3.1 Other incomplete records problems revolve around the relationship between sales, cost of sales and gross profit: in other words, they are based on reconstructing a trading account. Bear in mind the crucial formula:

		Example %
	Cost of sales	100
Plus	Gross profit	25
Equals	Sales	125

3.2 Gross profit may be expressed *either* as a percentage of cost of sales *or* as a percentage of sales.

- In the example, gross profit is 25% of cost of sales (ie 25/100). The terminology is *a 25% mark-up*.

- Gross profit can also be expressed as 20% of sales (ie 25/125). The terminology is *a 20% gross margin* or *gross profit percentage*.

3.3 Once again, there may be an unknown figure to calculate. For example, the figure of cash sales may need to be derived; or stock may have been lost or stolen. In the latter case, the procedure is usually to work out the cost of sales using a gross margin calculation, and then to use the formula:

> Cost of sales = opening stock + purchases - closing stock

The value of the missing stock can be entered as a balancing figure.

7: INCOMPLETE RECORDS

QUESTIONS

1 Which one of the following formulae may be used to calculate gross profit?

- A Net profit plus expenses
- B Cost of goods sold less purchases
- C Sales plus cost of goods sold
- D Opening stock plus purchases less closing stock

Circle your answer

A B C D

2 The following information is available in respect of a sole trader:

	£
Net profit for the year	7,000
Drawings	9,000
Capital at the end of the year	31,000

There were no new injections of capital during the year.

What was the trader's opening capital?

- A £16,000
- B £29,000
- C £33,000
- D £47,000

Circle your answer

A B C D

3 Mr Harmon does not keep full accounting records, but the following information is available in respect of his accounting year ended 31 December 19X9:

	£
Cash purchases in year	3,900
Cash paid for goods supplied on credit	27,850
Creditors at 1 January 19X9	970
Creditors at 31 December 19X9	720

In his trading account for 19X9, what will be Harmon's figure for purchases?

- A £27,600
- B £31,500
- C £31,750
- D £32,000

Circle your answer

A B C D

7: INCOMPLETE RECORDS

Data for questions 4 - 5

This is an extract from a business's trading account:

	£	£
Sales		300,000
Opening stock	24,000	
Purchases	229,000	
	253,000	
Closing stock	28,000	
		225,000

4 The gross profit as a percentage of cost of sales is:

  A   25%
  B   33⅓ %
  C   66⅔ %
  D   75%

Circle your answer

A   B   C   D

5 The gross profit as a percentage of sales is:

  A   25%
  B   33⅓ %
  C   66⅔ %
  D   75%

Circle your answer

A   B   C   D

6 If sales are £8,000 and the gross profit percentage is 20% what is the cost of sales?

  A   £1,600
  B   £2,000
  C   £6,000
  D   £6,400

Circle your answer

A   B   C   D

7: INCOMPLETE RECORDS

7 If sales are £70,000 and the gross mark-up is 40% what is the gross profit?

A £20,000
B £28,000
C £42,000
D £50,000

Circle your answer

A   B   C   D

8 Harriet has opening stock of £27,200 and makes purchases during the year of £314,500. She removes goods costing £570 for her own use. The business achieves a constant mark-up of 20% on cost and records sales for the year of £364,800.

What is the cost of Harriet's closing stock?

A £37,130
B £37,700
C £49,290
D £49,860

Circle your answer

A   B   C   D

9 A sweet shop makes purchases of £10,124 and sales of £13,260. The proprietor's children take goods costing £243 without paying for them. Closing stock was valued at its cost of £1,120 and the gross margin achieved was a constant 30% on sales.

What was the cost of the opening stock?

A £278
B £521
C £1,196
D £1,439

Circle your answer

A   B   C   D

10 Heather's stock at 1 January 19X5 was valued at cost of £18,000. Her budgets for 19X5 include the following estimates:

	£
Sales	112,000
Stock at 31 December 19X5	24,000

If Heather achieves a constant gross mark-up of 25% on cost, what is her estimated figure for purchases in 19X5?

A £78,000
B £83,600
C £90,000
D £95,600

Circle your answer

A   B   C   D

7: INCOMPLETE RECORDS

11 Harry has budgeted sales for the coming year of £175,000. He achieves a constant gross mark-up of 40% on cost. He plans to reduce his stock level by £13,000 over the year.

What will Harry's purchases be for the year?

A £92,000
B £112,000
C £118,000
D £138,000

Circle your answer

A   B   C   D

12 Hengist, a sole trader, has calculated that his cost of sales for the year is £144,000. His sales figure for the year includes an amount of £2,016 being the amount paid by Hengist himself into the business bank account for goods withdrawn for private use. The figure of £2,016 was calculated by adding a mark-up of 12% to the cost of the goods. His gross profit percentage on all other goods sold was 20%.

What is the total figure of sales for the year?

A £172,656
B £177,750
C £179,766
D £180,000

Circle your answer

A   B   C   D

13 Horsa's sales follow a seasonal pattern. Monthly sales in the final quarter of the year are twice as high as during other periods. He also benefits from a higher mark-up during the final quarter: an average of 25% on cost compared with 20% during the rest of the year.

Horsa's sales in 19X9 totalled £210,000. What was the amount of his gross profit?

A £36,750
B £37,800
C £39,667
D £46,200

Circle your answer

A   B   C   D

14 Hyman's opening stock is £28,520. Purchases and sales for 19X9 were £112,900 and £182,000 respectively. The gross margin is a constant 40% on sales. On 31 December 19X9 a fire destroyed all the stock on Hyman's premises, except for sundry small items with a cost of £480.

What was the cost of the stock destroyed?

A £10,940
B £11,420
C £31,740
D £32,220

Circle your answer

A   B   C   D

81

7: INCOMPLETE RECORDS

15 Happy's stock on 1 January 19X5 cost £14,300 and his creditors were £3,750. During the year his sales amounted to £174,000, earning an average mark-up of 33⅓% on cost. He paid £133,650 to suppliers during the year and creditors' balances at 31 December 19X5 totalled £4,900. On the same date his shop was burgled and all his stock was stolen.

What was the cost of the stolen stock?

- A £16,300
- B £18,600
- C £30,800
- D £33,100

Circle your answer

| A | B | C | D |

16 Hammett is a sole trader. The following information is available in respect of his accounting year ended 31 December 19X6:

	Opening balances £	Closing balances £
Debtors	4,300	5,500
Creditors	2,800	5,100
Stock	6,300	2,500

Hammett's bank statements for the year show payments to creditors of £46,300 and receipts from debtors of £72,500.

What is Hammett's gross profit percentage?

- A 28.9%
- B 30.9%
- C 35.1%
- D 40.6%

Circle your answer

| A | B | C | D |

17 Huxley is a retailer whose sales are all on cash terms. During 19X6 his bank account shows cash banked of £47,650, which included £220 from his own private funds. Huxley estimates that he drew about £150 per month from the till to cover private living expenses, and he also paid casual wages of £20 per week in cash. If the cash in the till amounted to £310 on 1 January 19X6 and £260 on 31 December 19X6, what is Huxley's sales figure for the year?

- A £47,380
- B £50,220
- C £50,320
- D £50,440

Circle your answer

| A | B | C | D |

7: INCOMPLETE RECORDS

18 Horton's cost of sales in 19X7 was £35,700. He achieves a gross profit percentage of 40%. All his sales are for cash, and his till balances at the beginning and end of the year were £175 and £95 respectively. Cash paid into the bank during the year amounted to £40,100. Cash expenses paid from till receipts were £2,150 for the year, but Horton cannot remember the amount of his own cash drawings.

His drawings amounted to:

A £7,810
B £17,170
C £17,330
D £21,630

Circle your answer

A   B   C   D

19 The bookkeeper of Leggit Ltd has disappeared. There is no cash in the till and theft is suspected. It is known that the cash balance at the beginning of the year was £240. Since then, total sales have amounted to £41,250. Credit customers owed £2,100 at the beginning of the year and owe £875 now. Cheques banked from credit customers have totalled £24,290. Expenses paid from the till receipts amount to £1,850 and cash receipts of £9,300 have been lodged in the bank.

How much has the bookkeeper stolen during the period?

A £7,275
B £9,125
C £12,155
D £16,575

Circle your answer

A   B   C   D

20 Hayley's debtors at 1 January 19X7 and 31 December 19X7 were £2,150 and £3,200 respectively. Cheques received from debtors during the year totalled £37,400. Hayley also makes cash sales: till receipts banked during the year totalled £13,950 after cash payments had been made in respect of sundry expenses. Her cost of sales for the year was £50,000 and she achieves a constant mark-up of 20%.

If the balances in the till at 1 January 19X7 and 31 December 19X7 were £235 and £195 respectively what was the amount of sundry expenses paid in cash?

A £7,560
B £7,640
C £9,740
D £10,140

Circle your answer

A   B   C   D

CHAPTER 8

INCOME AND EXPENDITURE ACCOUNTS

> This chapter covers the following topics:
> - The accounts of non-trading organisations
> - Members' subscriptions

1. The accounts of non-trading organisations

1.1 In many respects, the accounts of non-trading organisations are no different from those of a sole trader. Use of the accruals concept to match income with related expenditure is still necessary. Assets and liabilities are listed in a balance sheet in just the same way.

1.2 But there are some differences.

- Non-trading organisations do not exist to make profits. The difference between income and matching expenditure is therefore referred to as a surplus or deficit, rather than as a profit or loss. Similarly, the income statement itself is called an income and expenditure account, not a profit and loss account.

- The proprietorship of the organisation is referred to as the accumulated fund, not as capital. There may also be funds for other designated purposes, such as a building fund. Any such fund will be represented by specific assets, and these may increase each year as income is earned on them.

- There is no separate trading account. Within the income and expenditure account, income and expenditure relating to the same activity are netted off against each other.

1.3 The sources of income for a club or society may be more varied than for a trading concern. They might include:

- members' subscriptions (joining fees, annual subscriptions and life membership)
- "profits" from bar sales
- "profits" from social events, such as dinner dances
- receipts from gaming machines
- interest received on investments

1.4 The list above shows that even a non-profit-making organisation may have *some* trading activities, of which the most common is the operation of a members' bar. Any profit earned on such activities is normally shown as a single item of income in the income and expenditure account. As usual, it is common to deduct any related costs (eg a barman's wages) before disclosing the net profit in the income and expenditure account.

8: INCOME AND EXPENDITURE ACCOUNTS

2. Members' subscriptions

2.1 Some clubs and societies charge an initial joining fee to new members. Such fees are simply credited to income in the year of receipt.

2.2 Annual subscriptions are usually payable in advance. It is common to adopt a subscription year which coincides with the accounting year. However, some clubs require members to pay subscriptions in respect of a calendar year, even though the accounting year may end on, say, 31 March.

2.3 There are two problems in applying the accruals concept to members' subscriptions.

- Should the concept be applied at all? Subscriptions are not legally enforceable (a member can simply leave) and many clubs take the prudent view that they should not be credited to income until they are actually received. In this case, no debtor for subscriptions receivable will appear in the balance sheet.

- There is also the arithmetical problem of calculating the accruals and prepayments. Some members pay in advance; some pay in arrears; and finally the subscription year may differ from the accounting year. These calculations are a favourite topic with examiners and you must read the question very carefully to get the right result.

2.4 There are two common methods of accounting for life membership subscriptions.

- Credit the money to a life membership fund. Invest the funds in, say, a building society. Credit any interest received to the income and expenditure account. On the death of the member, transfer the amount of the life membership subscription to the accumulated fund.

- Credit the money to a life membership fund. Transfer the total gradually to income and expenditure account by a process of annual "amortisation".

8: INCOME AND EXPENDITURE ACCOUNTS

QUESTIONS

1 A club takes credit for subscriptions when they become due. On 1 January 19X5 arrears of subscriptions amounted to £38 and subscriptions paid in advance were £72. On 31 December 19X5 the amounts were £48 and £80 respectively. Subscription receipts during the year were £790.

In the income and expenditure account for 19X5 the income from subscriptions would be shown as:

- A £748
- B £788
- C £790
- D £792

Circle your answer

A   B   C   D

2 A club takes no credit for subscriptions due until they are received. On 1 January 19X5 arrears of subscriptions amounted to £24 and subscriptions paid in advance were £14. On 31 December 19X5 the amounts were £42 and £58 respectively. Subscription receipts during the year were £1,024.

In the income and expenditure account for 19X5 the income from subscriptions would be shown as:

- A £956
- B £980
- C £998
- D £1,050

Circle your answer

A   B   C   D

Data for questions 3 and 4

The following balances were extracted from the books of the Grand Slam Bridge Club as at 31 December 19X5:

	£
Tables and chairs	380
Playing cards and other accessories	102
Stock of reference books	130
Subscriptions in advance	80
Subscriptions in arrears	27
Life membership fund	300
Deficit for the year	117

Life membership funds are accounted for by crediting them to a life membership account, where they remain until the death of the member.

The only movement on the life membership account in 19X5 arose from the death of one of the five life members during the year. His subscription had been transferred to accumulated fund before the above balances were extracted.

8: INCOME AND EXPENDITURE ACCOUNTS

3 What was the balance on the accumulated fund at 31 December 19X5?

A £184
B £259
C £365
D £559

Circle your answer

A   B   C   D

4 What was the balance on the accumulated fund at 1 January 19X5?

A £217
B £301
C £316
D £376

Circle your answer

A   B   C   D

Data for questions 5 and 6

A club's bar stocks at 1 January 19X5 cost £3,750. During the year to 31 December 19X5, cash receipts from customers of £28,340 were lodged in the bank. The barman's wages of £50 per week were paid from till receipts. Bar purchases during the year amounted to £21,200. Bar prices are fixed so as to achieve a uniform gross profit percentage of 40%.

5 Calculate the cost of bar stock at 31 December 19X5.

A £2,850
B £6,386
C £7,946
D £9,506

Circle your answer

A   B   C   D

6 What is the net profit on bar trading disclosed in the club's income and expenditure account for 19X5?

A £9,776
B £12,376
C £15,964
D £18,564

Circle your answer

A   B   C   D

8: INCOME AND EXPENDITURE ACCOUNTS

7 For many years, life membership of the Tipton Poetry Association cost £100, but with effect from 1 January 19X5 the rate has been increased to £120. The balance on the life membership fund at 31 December 19X4 was £3,780 and membership details at that date were as follows:

	No of members
Joined more than 19 years ago	32
Joined within the last 19 years	64
	96

The Association's accounting policy is to release life subscriptions to income over a period of 20 years beginning with the year of enrolment.

During 19X5, four new members were enrolled and one other member (who had joined in 19X1) died.

What is the balance on the life membership fund at 31 December 19X5?

- A £3,591
- B £3,841
- C £3,916
- D £4,047

Circle your answer

A   B   C   D

8 The following information relates to a sports club:

	£
19X4 subscriptions unpaid at beginning of 19X5	410
19X4 subscriptions received during 19X5	370
19X5 subscriptions received during 19X5	6,730
19X6 subscriptions received during 19X5	1,180
19X5 subscriptions unpaid at end of 19X5	470

The club takes credit for subscription income when it becomes due, but takes a prudent view of overdue subscriptions. What amount should be credited to the income and expenditure account for 19X5?

- A £7,200
- B £7,240
- C £7,610
- D £8,380

Circle your answer

A   B   C   D

Data for questions 9 and 10

On 1 January 19X5 a club owed its suppliers £435 in respect of bar stocks; on 31 December 19X5 the amount was £363. The cash book showed payments to suppliers of £5,685 during the year. Opening stock amounts to £390. Bar sales are mostly on cash terms, though IOUs are occasionally accepted from members. IOUs outstanding at 1 January 19X5 amounted to £12; on 31 December the figure was £8. The cash book shows that till receipts lodged in the bank during the year amounted to £6,064, but this was after paying the barman's wages of £20 per week in cash. Bar prices are fixed so as to earn a constant mark-up of 25% on cost.

8: INCOME AND EXPENDITURE ACCOUNTS

9 Calculate the cost of closing stock at 31 December 19X5.

A £323
B £678
C £1,155
D £1,987

Circle your answer

A   B   C   D

10 What is the net profit on bar trading disclosed in the club's income and expenditure account for 19X5?

A £380
B £1,420
C £4,640
D £5,680

Circle your answer

A   B   C   D

11 A club with 200 members has an accounting year end of 31 March, but charges subscriptions in respect of calendar years. Subscriptions are due in advance each 1 January and the club duly takes credit for them as soon as they are due. Separate accounts are maintained for subscriptions due but unpaid and subscriptions received in advance.

The subscription rate for calendar year 19X6 is £50 per member. Between 1 January and 31 March 19X6 subscription receipts amount to £9,200. In the balance sheet at 31 March 19X6 what is the amount for subscriptions received in advance?

A £2,500
B £6,700
C £6,900
D £7,500

Circle your answer

A   B   C   D

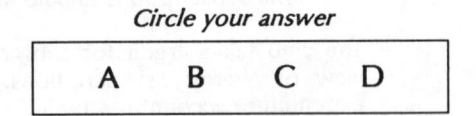

Data for questions 12 and 13

The Anthropology Club makes up its accounts to 30 September each year and has 500 members at any time.

Subscriptions are payable in respect of calendar years at a rate of £75 for 19X7 and £85 for 19X8. The club takes credit for them as soon as they are due.

At 30 September 19X7 four members were in arrears with their 19X7 subscriptions. One year later this amount had been settled but two members were in arrears with their 19X8 subscriptions. Separate accounts are maintained for subscriptions due but unpaid and subscriptions received in advance.

Subscription receipts during 19X8 totalled £42,630.

8: INCOME AND EXPENDITURE ACCOUNTS

12 At 30 September 19X7 what amount should be shown in the club's balance sheet as 'subscriptions in arrears'?

- A £75
- B £150
- C £225
- D £300

Circle your answer

A   B   C   D

13 What amount should be credited to the club's income and expenditure account for the year ending 30 September 19X8?

- A £31,875
- B £41,250
- C £42,533
- D £42,660

Circle your answer

A   B   C   D

Data for questions 14 - 17

The Risky Sports Association was established in 19X1.

The following details are available in respect of life members.

Year of admission	Number of life members admitted	Life membership fee per member	Life members dying in 19X2	in 19X3	in 19X4	in 19X5
19X2	12	£96	2	4	3	1
19X3	7	£108	-	1	3	2
19X4	9	£120	-	-	2	5
19X5	10	£132	-	-	-	2

The Association's accounting policy is to credit life membership subscriptions to a life membership fund, from which they are transferred to income and expenditure account over a three year period beginning in the year of payment. On the death of a member any remaining balance relating to him is transferred immediately to the accumulated fund.

14 What is the amount of life membership subscriptions disclosed in the income and expenditure account for 19X3?

- A £252
- B £408
- C £536
- D £636

Circle your answer

A   B   C   D

91

8: INCOME AND EXPENDITURE ACCOUNTS

15 What is the amount of life membership subscriptions disclosed in the income and expenditure account for 19X5?

    A   £440
    B   £468
    C   £532
    D   £828

Circle your answer

A   B   C   D

16 What is the amount of the transfer to accumulated fund in respect of members dying in 19X4?

    A   £240
    B   £268
    C   £552
    D   £852

Circle your answer

A   B   C   D

17 What is the balance on the life membership fund at the end of 19X5?

    A   £784
    B   £1,056
    C   £1,252
    D   £1,596

Circle your answer

A   B   C   D

18 On 1 July 19X6 the balance sheet of the Crazy Golf Club included the following amounts:

	£
Building fund assets	
2,000 10% preference shares of £1 each in Eagle plc	1,200
Building society account	850
	2,050
Building fund	2,050

During the year the club received a donation towards the building fund of £450 and also received £120 interest on the building society account.

What is the balance on the building fund account at 30 June 19X7?

    A   £2,500
    B   £2,620
    C   £2,740
    D   £2,820

Circle your answer

A   B   C   D

8: INCOME AND EXPENDITURE ACCOUNTS

19 At 1 January 19X5 the building fund of a club was represented by the following assets:

	£
£3,000 12% convertible loan stock at cost	4,200
Quoted shares at cost	6,400
Bank deposit account	1,120
	11,720

During 19X5 dividends received on the quoted shares represented a yield of 9% on cost, while deposit account interest amounted to £94.

The fund is boosted each year by a transfer of £500 from the income and expenditure account and a corresponding transfer of cash from the club's main bank account to the building fund deposit account.

What was the balance on the building fund account at 31 December 19X5?

A   £12,890
B   £13,250
C   £13,394
D   £13,750

Circle your answer

A   B   C   D

Data for questions 20 and 21

The following balances were taken from a club's books of account at 31 December 19X5:

	£
Premises	4,200
Furniture and accessories	512
Reference books	175
Subscriptions in advance	144
Subscriptions in arrears	60
Cash at bank	112
Life membership fund	1,200
Special activities fund	800
Deficit for the year	275

The deficit for the year is stated *after* the annual transfer of £200 to the special activities fund. An amount of £220 was transferred during 19X5 from the life membership fund to the accumulated fund in respect of life members who died during the year.

8: INCOME AND EXPENDITURE ACCOUNTS

20 What was the balance on the accumulated fund at 31 December 19X5?

- A £2,695
- B £2,715
- C £2,915
- D £3,083

Circle your answer

A B C D

21 What was the balance on the accumulated fund at 1 January 19X5?

- A £2,770
- B £2,860
- C £2,970
- D £3,190

Circle your answer

A B C D

CHAPTER 9

MANUFACTURING ACCOUNTS

> This chapter covers the following topics:
> - The main sections of a manufacturing account
> - Factory profit and transfer pricing

1. The main sections of a manufacturing account

1.1 Most businesses produce a trading account which compares the revenue earned from selling goods with the cost of the goods sold. This provides a good indication of how successful the company has been in its trading operations. In the case of a retail company which sells goods previously purchased from other businesses this may well be the most important accounting information required.

1.2 The situation is slightly more complicated in the case of a manufacturing business. Here there are two main aspects in the company's performance: the effectiveness and economy of its production operations, and the success of its trading activities. The second aspect is still covered by the production of a trading account, but the first requires a different accounting statement: a manufacturing account.

1.3 A manufacturing account aims to show the cost of producing finished goods stock. The elements included in manufacturing cost are arranged in a logical order to provide the format of a manufacturing account.

- The account begins with the cost of *raw materials* consumed in the period: opening stock plus purchases (including carriage inwards) less closing stock.

- The cost of *direct labour* is then added to arrive at the *prime cost* of production.

- The next step is the calculation of *factory overheads*.

- Finally, there is an adjustment in respect of *work in progress* (WIP). Opening WIP has been used up during the year and is therefore added to the cost of producing finished goods; the cost of closing WIP is a deduction from the factory cost of finished goods.

1.4 The factory cost of finished goods produced may then be transferred to the trading account as part of the cost of goods sold. Alternatively, there may be a notional loading in respect of manufacturing profit before this transfer takes place (see below).

9: MANUFACTURING ACCOUNTS

2. Factory profit and transfer pricing

2.1 For the purposes of management information it is often convenient to work out how much of the profit earned by a business arises from its pure trading operations (ie selling finished goods) and how much arises from its manufacturing operations. It may seem strange to calculate a profit on manufacturing, because of course the factory does not 'sell' finished goods to the warehouse in the normal sense. Both factory and warehouse belong to the same business and no cash changes hands.

2.2 Even so the concept of a 'profit' on manufacturing makes sense if it is thought of as the saving made by a business by virtue of producing its own goods rather than buying them in from outside.

2.3 For this reason, some businesses extend the manufacturing account beyond the 'factory cost of finished goods produced' by adding on an amount described as *factory profit*. This leads to a grand total of 'transfer price of finished goods produced' which is included in the trading account.

2.4 The gross profit disclosed by the trading account is then, appropriately, the gross profit on pure trading operations. The factory profit must then be added back in the profit and loss account: we have effectively debited manufacturing account and credited profit and loss account so that the net effect on reported profits is nil.

9: MANUFACTURING ACCOUNTS

QUESTIONS

1 Which one of the following costs would *not* be shown as a factory overhead in a manufacturing account?

A The cost of insurance on a factory
B The cost of an extension to a factory
C The cost of depreciation on a factory
D The cost of rent on a factory

Circle your answer

A   B   C   D

2 Which one of the following costs would be included in the calculation of prime cost in a manufacturing account?

A Factory rent
B Office wages
C Direct production wages
D Depreciation on machinery

Circle your answer

A   B   C   D

3 Which one of the following costs would be included in the calculation of prime cost in a manufacturing account?

A Cost of transporting raw materials from suppliers' premises

B Wages of factory workers engaged in machine maintenance

C Depreciation of lorries used for deliveries to customers

D Cost of indirect production materials

Circle your answer

A   B   C   D

4 A company's usage of raw materials during a year was £35,800. Direct labour costs amounted to £53,400, production overheads to £14,800 and administration overheads to £10,200. Opening work in progress was £3,600 and closing work in progress was £4,700.

In the company's manufacturing account, factory cost of finished goods produced is:

A £102,900
B £105,100
C £113,100
D £115,300

Circle your answer

A   B   C   D

9: MANUFACTURING ACCOUNTS

Data for questions 5 - 7

The following details are available in respect of a company's manufacturing operations during 19X5:

		£
Work in progress:	opening stock	42,920
	closing stock	39,610
Raw materials:	opening stock	12,940
	purchases in year	213,680
	closing stock	14,550
Carriage inwards		3,970
Carriage outwards		4,200
Wages and salaries:	factory supervisor	12,490
	direct production staff	96,380
	other factory staff	18,330
	administration staff	21,520
Other factory costs		63,310

The company transfers goods from factory to warehouse at a price which represents a profit to the factory of 15% on the transfer price.

5 What is the prime cost of production in 19X5?

A £312,420
B £312,650
C £314,030
D £324,910

Circle your answer

A   B   C   D

6 What is the factory cost of finished goods produced in 19X5?

A £403,240
B £409,860
C £428,960
D £435,580

Circle your answer

A   B   C   D

9: MANUFACTURING ACCOUNTS

7 What is the factory profit on goods transferred to the warehouse in 19X5?

A £60,486
B £61,479
C £71,160
D £72,328

Circle your answer

A B C D

Data for questions 8 - 9

The factory cost of finished goods produced by a manufacturing company in 19X6 was £780,000. The opening stock of finished goods had been valued at £57,375, and the closing stock at £51,300, both inclusive of factory profit of 8% on cost. Goods are sold at a mark-up of 20% above the transfer price from the factory.

8 What is the sales figure for the year?

A £848,475
B £942,750
C £943,290
D £1,018,170

Circle your answer

A B C D

9 What figure would be included in the profit and loss account in respect of unrealised profit in stock?

A £450
B £486
C £3,800
D £4,250

Circle your answer

A B C D

9: MANUFACTURING ACCOUNTS

Data for questions 10 - 11

A company's manufacturing operations take place in two departments: assembly and finishing. Wages costs in these departments during 19X6 amounted to £120,000 and £80,000 respectively. Manufacturing overheads incurred during the year were £320,000. These are to be apportioned between the two departments in proportion to their wages costs. Departmental overheads are then apportioned to the company's two product lines as follows:

	Assembly	Finishing
Product Y	60%	30%
Product Z	40%	70%

10 Calculate the overhead cost attributable to product Y during the year.

- A £96,000
- B £153,600
- C £192,000
- D £249,600

Circle your answer

A   B   C   D

11 Calculate the overhead cost attributable to product Z during the year.

- A £128,000
- B £166,400
- C £224,000
- D £270,400

Circle your answer

A   B   C   D

Data for questions 12 - 13

A manufacturing company transfers finished goods from factory to warehouse at cost plus 5%. At 31 December its stocks of finished goods, valued at transfer prices, have been as follows:

19X5	£4,620
19X6	£5,460
19X7	£3,780

9: MANUFACTURING ACCOUNTS

12 In the profit and loss account for the year ended 31 December 19X6 the adjustment for unrealised profit should be:

- A £42 debit
- B £42 credit
- C £40 debit
- D £40 credit

Circle your answer

A   B   C   D

13 In the profit and loss account for the year ended 31 December 19X7 the adjustment for unrealised profit should be:

- A £84 debit
- B £84 credit
- C £80 debit
- D £80 credit

Circle your answer

A   B   C   D

14 Many manufacturing companies transfer goods from factory to warehouse at a price which includes a mark-up on production cost. Once the mark-up has been calculated for a year's production, what double entry is needed to bring it into the books of account?

- A *Debit*   Profit and loss account
     Credit   Manufacturing account

- B *Debit*   Manufacturing account
     Credit   Profit and loss account

- C *Debit*   Manufacturing account
     Credit   Provision for unrealised profit

- D *Debit*   Profit and loss account
     Credit   Provision for unrealised profit

Circle your answer

A   B   C   D

Data for questions 15 - 16

The following balances with respect to stock have been extracted from the books of a small manufacturer as at 31 December.

	31 December 19X8 £	31 December 19X7 £
Consumable stores (used in manufacturing operations)	2,200	1,466
Raw materials	76,500	59,500
Work in progress	68,000	42,500
Finished goods (at transfer price)	87,975	58,650
Delivery cases	1,408	938

Factory output is transferred to the trading account at factory cost plus 25% factory profit.

101

9: MANUFACTURING ACCOUNTS

15 What entry is required in the profit and loss account for the year ended 31 December 19X8 in respect of unrealised profit?

  A £5,865 debit
  B £5,865 credit
  C £7,331 debit
  D £7,331 credit

Circle your answer

| A | B | C | D |

16 What aggregate values will be included in respect of closing stock in the manufacturing account for the year ended 31 December 19X8 and in the balance sheet as at that date before adjusting for unrealised profit?

  A £76,500 and £232,475 respectively
  B £144,500 and £236,083 respectively
  C £146,700 and £236,083 respectively
  D £148,108 and £232,475 respectively

Circle your answer

| A | B | C | D |

Data for questions 17 - 19

The following details are available in respect of a manufacturing company's activities during 19X5:

	£
Opening stocks at 1 January 19X5:	
Raw materials	22,750
Work in progress	37,610
Raw material purchases	151,500
Direct labour	87,200
Depreciation of plant	12,900
Other overheads	125,800
Carriage inwards	3,410
Carriage outwards	5,220
Closing stocks at 31 December 19X5:	
Raw materials	18,630
Work in progress	41,260

"Other overheads" are to be apportioned on the basis of: factory 30%; finished goods warehouse 40%; administration 30%. The total of other overheads does not yet include an accrual of £4,200 in respect of rent. Goods are transferred from factory to warehouse at a mark-up of 25%. Units of production output during 19X5 were 9,000.

9: MANUFACTURING ACCOUNTS

17 What was the prime cost of production in 19X5?

- A £242,110
- B £242,820
- C £246,230
- D £248,040

Circle your answer

A B C D

18 What was the factory cost of one unit of finished production in 19X5?

- A £32.58
- B £32.72
- C £40.90
- D £42.83

Circle your answer

A B C D

19 What was the factory profit on goods transferred to the warehouse in 19X5?

- A £58,896
- B £73,305
- C £73,620
- D £96,370

Circle your answer

A B C D

20 The factory cost of finished goods produced by a manufacturing company in 19X5 was £638,400. Opening and closing stocks of finished goods were £44,800 and £50,400 respectively, each valuation including a factory profit of 12% on production cost. Goods are sold to customers at a mark-up of 25% on production cost.

What is the sales figure for 19X5?

- A £695,990
- B £706,250
- C £791,750
- D £791,840

Circle your answer

A B C D

103

CHAPTER 10

PARTNERSHIP ACCOUNTS

> This chapter covers the following topics:
>
> - The partnership agreement
> - Capital accounts and current accounts
> - The appropriation account
> - Changes in the structure of a partnership

1. The partnership agreement

1.1 A partnership is an arrangement between two or more individuals in which they undertake to share the risks and rewards of a joint business operation. The financial arrangements agreed between the partners are often set out in a formal document called a *partnership agreement*. This might include clauses relating to:

- the amount of capital to be provided by each partner

- the division of profits between partners. Profits might be earned in the form of salaries, interest on capital and residual profit share. The agreement will usually specify a ratio (the profit sharing ratio) in which residual profits are to be shared by the partners.

1.2 In the absence of a formal agreement between the partners, certain rules laid down by the Partnership Act 1890 are presumed to apply instead. In such a case:

- residual profits are shared equally between the partners
- there are no partners' salaries
- partners receive no interest on the capital they invest in the business
- partners are entitled to interest of 5% per annum on any loans they advance to the business in excess of their agreed capital.

1.3 Don't forget that these terms only apply in the absence of any agreement to the contrary. In tackling the questions in this chapter you should look first of all for the details of a specific partnership agreement; only if none are given should you apply the provisions of the Partnership Act 1890.

2. Capital accounts and current accounts

2.1 The assets employed by a partnership are no different from those of a sole trader. But the capital side of a partnership's balance sheet is more complicated. It is usual to maintain both a capital account and a current account for each partner.

105

10: PARTNERSHIP ACCOUNTS

2.2 A partner's capital account shows any cash or other assets brought by him into the business. He will usually make an initial capital contribution when he joins the partnership, but there may also be further injections (or withdrawals) of capital later on.

2.3 While the balance on a partner's capital account is likely to remain stable for long periods, his current account balance will fluctuate more rapidly. He will draw money regularly from the business to support his living expenses and these drawings will be debited to his current account. But he will also be entitled to a share of the business profits and this will be credited to his current account at least annually.

3. The appropriation account

3.1 In the case of a sole trader, retained profits earned each year are simply added to his capital balance. With a partnership things are more complicated. After calculating the net profit earned by the business an appropriation account must be prepared to determine the allocation of profit between the partners.

3.2 To discourage excessive drawings partners often agree to charge themselves interest on any sums withdrawn from the business. Such interest is charged to the partner concerned (ie debited to his current account) and credited to the appropriation account, increasing the profit available for sharing between the partners.

3.3 The sum available for appropriation must now be shared amongst the partners and credited to their current accounts.

- Some partners may be entitled to a salary. This is credited to the partner concerned and taken out of the 'pool' available for appropriation.

- Partners may be entitled to interest on their capital account balances. Each partner is credited with the appropriate amount and again the 'pool' is reduced.

- Finally, the residual 'pool' of profits is shared amongst the partners in their profit sharing ratio.

4. Changes in the structure of a partnership

4.1 The structure of a firm may change if new partners are admitted or existing partners leave. This can cause accounting problems if the books of the partnership do not fully reflect the value of the business. Such a situation is very common: for example, few firms include the asset of goodwill in their books of account even though its value may be very material.

4.2 The usual solution is to make a temporary adjustment so that partners' capital accounts for the moment reflect the value of any intangible assets such as goodwill. Before the new partner is admitted or the existing partner leaves make the following entries:

10: PARTNERSHIP ACCOUNTS

Debit   Goodwill account (introducing the agreed value of goodwill into the partnership books)

Credit   Partners' capital accounts (giving each partner his share of the new asset. The split is based on profit sharing ratio)

4.3 At this stage it is clear how much is due to a retiring partner, or how much must be paid in by a new partner to acquire a share of the firm's goodwill. Appropriate entries can then be made to close off the retiring partner's account or to open the new partner's account.

4.4 Once this has been done, and the new partnership structure is in place, reverse the temporary adjustment as follows:

Debit   Partners' capital accounts (dividing the total between the partners in the new firm, in their agreed profit sharing ratio)

Credit   Goodwill account (removing the intangible asset from the books of account).

10: PARTNERSHIP ACCOUNTS

QUESTIONS

1 A partnership employs an inexperienced bookkeeper. He has written up the current account of one of the partners as follows:

CURRENT ACCOUNT

	£		£
Interest on capital	2,800	Balance b/f	270
Salary	1,500	Drawings	6,200
Balance c/f	10,870	Net profit	8,700
	15,170		15,170

The balance brought forward is entered correctly and the other entries are all correct in amount. However, the bookkeeper is not very sure of the difference between debits and credits.

What is the corrected balance carried forward?

- A A debit balance of £1,530
- B A debit balance of £6,530
- C A credit balance of £7,070
- D A credit balance of £16,470

Circle your answer

A   B   C   D

2 In the absence of a formal partnership agreement, which of the following is prescribed by the Partnership Act 1890?

- A Equal profit shares
- B Interest on capital
- C Interest on drawings
- D Partners' salaries

Circle your answer

A   B   C   D

3 Excluding certain professional firms, what is the normal limit on the number of partners in a partnership?

- A 5
- B 10
- C 15
- D 20

Circle your answer

A   B   C   D

10: PARTNERSHIP ACCOUNTS

4 A partner's private petrol bills have been treated as part of the partnership's motor vehicle expenses. Which of the following entries is necessary to correct the error?

- A *Debit* Drawings account
  Credit Motor vehicle expenses account

- B *Debit* Motor vehicles expenses account
  Credit Drawings account

- C *Debit* Motor vehicle expenses account
  Credit Capital account

- D *Debit* Capital account
  Credit Motor vehicle expenses account

Circle your answer

| A | B | C | D |

5 What double entry is necessary to reflect interest earned on partners' capital account balances?

- A *Debit* Partners' current accounts
  Credit Profit and loss appropriation account

- B *Debit* Profit and loss appropriation account
  Credit Partners' current accounts

- C *Debit* Profit and loss appropriation account
  Credit Cash

- D *Debit* Profit and loss appropriation account
  Credit Partners' capital accounts

Circle your answer

| A | B | C | D |

6 What double entry is necessary to reflect interest payable on partners' drawings?

- A *Debit* Partners' drawings accounts
  Credit Partners' current accounts

- B *Debit* Profit and loss appropriation account
  Credit Partners' drawings accounts

- C *Debit* Partners' drawings accounts
  Credit Interest payable account

- D *Debit* Partners' current accounts
  Credit Profit and loss appropriation account

Circle your answer

| A | B | C | D |

10: PARTNERSHIP ACCOUNTS

7 In the absence of any agreement to the contrary, the Partnership Act 1890 prescribes that salaries should be paid:

A to none of the partners
B to all of the partners in equal amounts
C only to partners active in the business
D only to partners with limited liability

Circle your answer

A   B   C   D

Data for questions 8 - 9

Faith, Hope and Charity are partners sharing residual profits in the ratio 3:2:1. The partnership agreement provides for interest on capital at the rate of 8% per annum and for a salary for Hope of £8,000 per annum. Net profit for 19X5 was £84,000 and the balances on partners' capital accounts during the year were: Faith £20,000; Hope £15,000; Charity £12,000.

8 Calculate Charity's share of residual profits for 19X5.

A £12,040
B £12,667
C £13,000
D £14,000

Circle your answer

A   B   C   D

9 Calculate the total of the appropriations credited to Hope's current account in 19X5.

A £24,080
B £28,000
C £33,280
D £33,333

Circle your answer

A   B   C   D

Data for questions 10 - 11

Publysh and Bedamd are partners in a bookshop business. They share residual profits in the ratio 3:2 after interest on partners' capital of 6% per annum and interest on partners' drawings of 10% per annum. Their capital balances throughout 19X6 were £8,000 and £6,000 respectively, and the average balances on their drawings accounts were £12,000 and £15,000. Net trading profit for 19X6 was £32,000.

10: PARTNERSHIP ACCOUNTS

10 Calculate the balance of residual profits available for appropriation in profit sharing ratio.

A £30,140
B £31,160
C £33,860
D £34,700

Circle your answer

A   B   C   D

11 Calculate the *net* amount of all the sums transferred from the appropriation account to the current account of Publysh.

A £19,116
B £19,596
C £20,316
D £20,796

Circle your answer

A   B   C   D

12 Alpha, Beta and Gamma are in partnership sharing residual profits in the ratio 2:2:1. Alpha has made a long-term loan to the partnership of £20,000 in addition to his fixed capital. The partnership agreement provides for interest on drawings at the rate of 10% per annum on the average amount withdrawn during the year. In other respects the provisions of the Partnership Act 1890 apply.

In 19X6 the net profit earned by the partnership, before charging any interest on the loan advanced by Alpha, was £38,700. Drawings (made evenly over the year) were: Alpha £8,600; Beta £9,200; Gamma £8,000.

Alpha's share of the residual profit for the year was:

A £14,564
B £15,596
C £16,112
D £16,596

Circle your answer

A   B   C   D

13 Nakert, Wheezy and Faggs are partners in a health food business, sharing profits and losses in the ratio 3:5:2. In 19X6 their net trading profit was £14,000. The partnership agreement provides for interest on partners' drawings at the rate of 10% per annum (based on the average balance on each partner's drawings account during the year), and for salaries of £6,000, £6,000 and £5,000 per annum respectively. Monthly drawings by the partners amount to £300, £320 and £250 respectively.

111

10: PARTNERSHIP ACCOUNTS

Calculate the *net* amount of all the sums transferred from the appropriation account to the current account of Wheezy.

A £1,239
B £4,431
C £4,569
D £5,808

Circle your answer

A   B   C   D

Data for questions 14 - 15

Nobby, Fingers and Swag are partners in a removals business. Their partnership agreement provides for annual salaries of £7,000 and £4,800 for Fingers and Swag respectively, interest on partners' drawings at 8% per annum irrespective of the date of withdrawal, and a profit sharing ratio of 2:5:3.

At the beginning of 19X8 capital account balances were:

Nobby	£30,000
Fingers	£12,000
Swag	£40,000

Net profit earned by the partnership in 19X8 was £30,000.

Drawings during 19X8 were

Nobby	£4,000
Fingers	£3,000
Swag	£3,000

14 What is Fingers's share of residual profit for 19X8?

A £9,100
B £9,500
C £16,100
D £16,500

Circle your answer

A   B   C   D

112

10: PARTNERSHIP ACCOUNTS

15 Assuming current account balances are cleared off to capital accounts at the end of each year, what is the balance on Fingers's capital account at the end of 19X8?

    A   £24,860
    B   £25,260
    C   £25,500
    D   £28,500

Circle your answer

    A   B   C   D

16 Tryit and Forsyze have been partners in a tailoring business for some years, sharing residual profits in the ratio 3:2. Forsyze wishes to retire from the business, leaving Tryit to continue with a new partner.

Forsyze's capital account stands at £21,000, while his current account has a debit balance of £1,400. Partnership goodwill (not reflected in the books) is valued at £8,000. Book values of tangible assets are about £3,000 less than their market values.

Calculate the amount due to Forsyze from the business on his retirement.

    A   £19,600
    B   £24,000
    C   £26,200
    D   £26,800

Circle your answer

    A   B   C   D

17 Minnie, Microw and Mayne have been partners for some years in a computer hardware business, sharing residual profits in the ratio 4:3:3. Their balance sheet at 30 June 19X5 showed the following:

	Minnie £	Microw £	Mayne £	Total £
Capital accounts	24,000	18,000	15,000	57,000
Current accounts	3,500	4,200	7,300	15,000
	27,500	22,200	22,300	72,000
Net tangible assets				72,000

Mayne wishes to retire and for this purpose goodwill is to be valued at £12,000 and certain tangible assets are to be revalued upwards by £5,000. Mayne is to take with him his company car at its book value of £4,800 and the rest of the money owing to him is left in the business on a loan account.

What is the balance on Mayne's loan account after these transactions are completed?

    A   £17,500
    B   £19,000
    C   £21,100
    D   £22,600

Circle your answer

    A   B   C   D

10: PARTNERSHIP ACCOUNTS

18 Luck and Flaw commence trading as puppet manufacturers on 1 January 19X6. They each contribute capital of £8,000 and agree to share profits equally. Business is slow for the first few months and the net profits are only £3,000 in the period to 30 June 19X6. On that date they are joined in partnership by Reagan who contributes capital of £10,000. The three partners are to share profits equally and they estimate that goodwill built up by Luck and Flaw in the first six months of trading has a value of £4,800. They do not wish to retain goodwill in the books of the business.

What is the balance on Reagan's capital account at 1 July 19X6?

A £8,400
B £9,200
C £9,400
D £10,000

Circle your answer

A   B   C   D

19 Bass, Guinness and Diamond were in partnership sharing profits in the ratio 3:2:1. The balances on their capital accounts as at 31 December 19X7 were:

	£
Bass	18,000
Guinness	10,000
Diamond	6,000

On 1 January 19X8 Mackeson was admitted to the partnership paying in £10,000 cash. The profit sharing ratio after the admission of Mackeson is 2:2:1:1. It is estimated that the business could be sold for £12,000 more than the book value of the net assets. After the necessary adjustments relating to the admission of Mackeson, the balances on the partners' capital accounts would be:

A Bass £20,000   Guinness £10,000
   Diamond £6,000   Mackeson £8,000

B Bass £20,000   Guinness £10,000
   Diamond £6,000   Mackeson £10,000

C Bass £18,000   Guinness £10,000
   Diamond £6,000   Mackeson £10,000

D Bass £18,000   Guinness £10,000
   Diamond £6,000   Mackeson £8,000

Circle your answer

A   B   C   D

10: PARTNERSHIP ACCOUNTS

Data for questions 20 - 23

Grub and Grime are in partnership as soap manufacturers, sharing profits in the ratio 3:1. They employ a works supervisor, Scrub, at an annual salary of £20,000.

On 30 June 19X5 Grub retires and Scrub is admitted to the partnership in his place. The new profit sharing arrangement excludes partners' salaries and divides residual profits as to Grime 3, Scrub 2. Scrub contributes initial capital of £12,000. The balance sheet at 31 December 19X4 showed Grub's and Grime's capital accounts as £38,000 and £29,000 respectively. The partners do not maintain separate current accounts. Net profits for 19X5 (before charging Scrub's salary or any loan interest) were £72,000 and these arose evenly over the year. Goodwill was valued at £9,000 on 30 June 19X5. Grub withdrew £20,000 in cash on leaving the business. The remaining balance due to him was left in the partnership on loan account at an interest rate of 10% per annum.

20 What is the balance transferred to Grub's loan account on 30 June 19X5?

- A £37,500
- B £44,250
- C £51,750
- D £64,250

Circle your answer

A   B   C   D

21 What is the balance on Grime's capital account on 31 December 19X5?

- A £50,348
- B £52,623
- C £53,950
- D £55,773

Circle your answer

A   B   C   D

22 What is the balance on Scrub's capital account on 1 July 19X5?

- A £8,400
- B £12,000
- C £15,600
- D £22,000

Circle your answer

A   B   C   D

10: PARTNERSHIP ACCOUNTS

23 What is the balance on Scrub's capital account on 31 December 19X5?

A £21,915
B £22,800
C £25,515
D £31,915

Circle your answer

A   B   C   D

Data for questions 24 - 25

Until 30 June 19X7 Alpha and Beta were in partnership together, while Gamma and Delta were another partnership. The balances on their capital accounts were:

| Alpha | £5,000 | Gamma | £6,000 |
| Beta | £3,000 | Delta | £2,000 |

On 30 June 19X7 Beta decided to retire. Alpha joined the firm of Gamma and Delta as a partner. In both the new firm and the two old firms partners share profits equally.

At the time of these changes, the tangible assets of Alpha and Beta were worth £4,000 *more* than their book values while those of Gamma and Delta were worth £6,000 *less* than book value. Neither firm had incorporated goodwill in its books, although that of Alpha and Beta was worth £10,000 and that of Gamma and Delta was worth £8,000.

Alpha paid off Beta in cash, and transferred the remaining assets into the firm of Gamma and Delta. No goodwill was to be shown in the books of the new firm.

24 What was the balance on Alpha's capital account after effecting these transactions?

A £2,000
B £6,000
C £9,333
D £12,000

Circle your answer

A   B   C   D

25 What is the value of the net tangible assets shown in the balance sheet of the new firm?

A £4,000
B £6,000
C £14,000
D £22,000

Circle your answer

A   B   C   D

116

10: PARTNERSHIP ACCOUNTS

26 When a partnership is dissolved a partner may agree to take over a non-monetary asset at a value in excess of its book value. The double entry in respect of this excess amount is:

A *Debit* Realisation account
   Credit Asset account

B *Debit* Bank
   Credit Asset account

C *Debit* Asset account
   Credit Purchase of business account

D *Debit* Asset account
   Credit Partners' accounts

Circle your answer

| A | B | C | D |

CHAPTER 11

COMPANY ACCOUNTS

> This chapter covers the following topics:
> - The capital structure of limited companies
> - The issue of shares
> - Interest and dividends

1. The capital structure of limited companies

1.1 The assets employed by a limited company will be similar to those of an unincorporated business: premises, plant and machinery, stock, debtors, cash and so on. The main difference that appears in a company's balance sheet is in the capital which finances the assets.

1.2 It is useful to begin by distinguishing two forms of long-term capital.

- *Loan capital*, often in the form of debentures, is money borrowed from outsiders. The company pays for the use of such funds by making interest payments. Eventually the funds themselves will be repaid to the lenders.

- *Share capital* is money subscribed by members of the company, who are also called shareholders. In return for the money they contribute they acquire a stake in the company. Shareholders earn a return on the money they invest in the form of dividends paid by the company, but their investment is not generally repayable: the cash stays in the company until it ceases to trade and is wound up.

1.3 Share capital can be further sub-divided.

- *Preference shares* are similar in nature to debentures in that their holders are entitled only to a fixed rate of return on their investment. For example, the holder of 1,000 6% £1 preference shares is entitled to an annual dividend of 1,000 x £1 x 6% = £60. Despite this similarity, the *difference* between preference shares and debentures is also important: the holder of preference shares is a member (part-owner) of the company, whereas a debenture holder is an external creditor of the company.

- *Ordinary* (or *equity*) *shares* entitle their holders to a full stake in the company. Any profits earned by the company, after paying interest on loan capital and dividends on preference share capital, belong to the ordinary shareholders.

1.4 A final distinction is between authorised and issued share capital.

- When a company is established, the original members draw up a 'constitution' for the new entity. This consists of two documents, a memorandum of association and articles of association. The memorandum lays down, amongst other things, a maximum amount of share capital that the company is empowered to issue. This is its *authorised* share capital.

- A company may not wish to issue all of its authorised capital at once. For example, a company with an authorised share capital of 1,000,000 ordinary shares of £1 each may decide that it needs only £200,000 in share capital for the time being. It might therefore issue only 200,000 shares, calling on subscribers to pay £1 for each of them. Its issued share capital would then be £200,000.

1.5 If a company is successful, it will make profits each year. Some of these profits may be paid out to shareholders in the form of dividends, but some may be retained within the business to finance future growth. Such retained profits are called *reserves*. Reserves are accumulated profits which belong to the equity shareholders but have not yet been paid out to them. Share capital (including preference shares) plus reserves are called *shareholders' funds*.

2. The issue of shares

2.1 Subject to the limit of its authorised share capital, a company may issue new shares at any time. It may call on investors to subscribe for the new shares at their market value, ie at the price they are thought to be worth, bearing in mind the financial strength of the company and its prospects for the future.

2.2 However, a company contemplating a new share issue will often turn first to its existing shareholders, offering them the chance to purchase new shares in proportion to the number they already hold. This is called a *rights issue*. For example, a company with 400,000 ordinary shares in issue and wishing to make a further issue of 160,000 shares might make a rights issue of 2 for 5, meaning that for every five shares already held a member is invited to subscribe for two more.

2.3 Unlike a rights issue, a *bonus issue* is not an issue of shares for cash. A company with a high level of reserves might decide to re-classify some of them as share capital by issuing shares at nil cost to existing shareholders. As with a rights issue, this must be done in proportion to members' existing shareholdings.

2.4 Shares must have a *nominal value*, ie they must be denominated as shares of 1p each or 50p each or £1 each or any other value. This nominal value is an arbitrary figure and is not related to the market value of the shares.

2.5 Shares may never be issued at a discount (ie at a price below their nominal value) but they may be issued at a premium (ie at a price above their nominal value). When this happens the premium received by the company is credited *not* to the share capital account, which is *always* maintained at the nominal value of the shares, but to a separate share premium account.

3. Interest and dividends

3.1 Providers of capital must be rewarded for their investment.

- Providers of loan capital (eg debenture holders) are paid interest.

- Providers of preference share capital receive a dividend at a fixed rate.

- Providers of ordinary share capital will also receive dividends but the level of payment may vary depending on the profitability of the company and the level of its cash resources.

3.2 Interest is paid to external creditors of the company and is therefore a charge against profits; dividends (including preference dividends) are paid to the owners of the company and are therefore an appropriation of profits.

3.3 The rate of a dividend may be expressed either as an amount per share, or as a percentage.

- If an amount per share is given, calculate how many shares are in issue. If a company's issued capital is £100,000 in 20p ordinary shares, there are 500,000 shares in issue.

- If a percentage is given, it relates to the *nominal* value of the *issued* share capital.

11: COMPANY ACCOUNTS

QUESTIONS

1 What is the meaning of the word "limited" in the name of a limited company?

- A The number of shareholders is limited to 50
- B The liability of the company for its own debts is limited
- C The liability of shareholders for the company's debts is limited
- D There is a limit on the amount of debts that the company can contract

Circle your answer

A   B   C   D

2 What is the meaning of a company's "authorised capital"?

- A The total amount of share capital it is allowed to issue
- B The amount of share capital it has issued
- C The amount of share capital for which payment has been received from subscribers
- D The maximum amount of loan capital prescribed by its articles of association

Circle your answer

A   B   C   D

3 Company law defines certain accounting and other records that a limited company must maintain. Which one of the following is *not* required to be maintained by a limited company in the retail trade?

- A A register of shareholders' 5% interests in the company
- B A register of debenture holders
- C A record of day-to-day cash inflows and outflows
- D A statement of stocks held at the year end

Circle your answer

A   B   C   D

11: COMPANY ACCOUNTS

4 When a shareholder in a limited company sells his shares to another private investor for less than he paid for them, the share capital of the company will:

- A fall by the nominal value of the shares
- B increase by the nominal value of the shares
- C increase by the amount received for the shares
- D remain unchanged

Circle your answer

A   B   C   D

5 Which one of the following does *not* form part of a limited company's equity capital?

- A Ordinary share capital
- B Preference share capital
- C Revaluation reserve
- D Debenture redemption reserve

Circle your answer

A   B   C   D

6 For which one of the following purposes is it *not* normally permissible to apply a share premium account?

- A Issuing fully paid bonus shares
- B Writing off preliminary expenses of formation
- C Writing off the premium payable on redemption of debentures
- D Writing off the premium payable on redemption of shares

Circle your answer

A   B   C   D

7 For which one of the following purposes is it permissible to apply a capital redemption reserve account?

- A Issuing fully paid bonus shares
- B Writing off preliminary expenses of formation
- C Writing off the premium payable on redemption of debentures
- D Writing off the premium payable on redemption of shares

Circle your answer

A   B   C   D

123

11: COMPANY ACCOUNTS

8 Which one of the following items would not appear in the appropriation account of a limited company?

A Ordinary dividend payable
B Preference dividend payable
C Debenture interest payable
D Transfer to general reserve

Circle your answer

A B C D

9 A company has an authorised share capital of £1,000,000, consisting of 25p ordinary shares. Its issued share capital consists of 500,000 shares.

A dividend of 2p per share is declared. The cash payable to shareholders amounts to:

A £10,000
B £20,000
C £40,000
D £80,000

Circle your answer

A B C D

10 A company has an authorised share capital of 10,000,000 50p ordinary shares. Its balance sheet shows allotted and fully paid capital of £2,000,000.

A dividend of 3p per share is declared. The cash payable to shareholders amounts to:

A £60,000
B £120,000
C £150,000
D £300,000

Circle your answer

A B C D

11 A company has an authorised share capital of 500,000 25p ordinary shares. Its issued share capital is 200,000 shares.

An ordinary dividend of 10% is declared. The cash payable to shareholders amounts to:

A £5,000
B £12,500
C £20,000
D £50,000

Circle your answer

A B C D

11: COMPANY ACCOUNTS

12 A company's issued share capital consists of £200,000 in 50p ordinary shares issued at a premium of 10p per share.

A dividend of 20% is declared. The cash payable to shareholders amounts to:

A £20,000
B £40,000
C £44,000
D £80,000

Circle your answer

A   B   C   D

13 A company has an authorised capital of 1,000,000 10p ordinary shares of which 800,000 are in issue. It is proposed to pay a dividend totalling £40,000. Which of the following expressions correctly describes the amount of the dividend?

A An ordinary dividend of 4%
B An ordinary dividend of 4p per share
C An ordinary dividend of 5%
D An ordinary dividend of 5p per share

Circle your answer

A   B   C   D

14 A company's authorised capital consists of 4,000,000 50p ordinary shares. The company pays a dividend of 3% and the total sum received by shareholders is £45,000. What is the figure of called up share capital appearing in the company's balance sheet?

A £1,500,000
B £2,000,000
C £3,000,000
D £4,000,000

Circle your answer

A   B   C   D

15 A company's share capital consists of 40,000 20p ordinary shares, which were all issued at a premium of 25%. The market value of the shares is currently 50p each. The figure for ordinary share capital appearing in the company's balance sheet would be:

A £8,000
B £10,000
C £18,000
D £20,000

Circle your answer

A   B   C   D

11: COMPANY ACCOUNTS

16 A company's issued capital consists of £50,000 in 8% £1 preference shares and £100,000 in 50p ordinary shares. Its net profit for the year was £184,000 and the directors wish to pay an ordinary dividend of 5p per share.

What is the company's retained profit for the year?

- A £170,000
- B £174,000
- C £175,000
- D £179,000

Circle your answer

A B C D

17 On 31 December 19X6 a company's issued share capital consisted of 25p ordinary shares, all of which had been issued at a premium of 20%. In the balance sheet the figure of called up share capital fully paid was £600,000.

During the year ended 31 December 19X7, the company made a bonus issue of 2 for 5. There were no other movements in share capital during the year. How many shares were in issue on 31 December 19X7?

- A 840,000
- B 2,800,000
- C 3,360,000
- D 4,000,000

Circle your answer

A B C D

18 On 31 December 19X4 a company's issued share capital consisted of £240,000 in 50p ordinary shares, all of which had been issued at a premium of 10%.

On 1 January 19X5 a bonus issue of 1 for 4 was made. On 1 March 19X5 a new issue for cash was made at a premium of 20p per share. The total cash received was £42,000.

In the balance sheet at 31 December 19X5 what is the figure for issued share capital?

- A £280,000
- B £330,000
- C £342,000
- D £660,000

Circle your answer

A B C D

11: COMPANY ACCOUNTS

Data for questions 19 - 21

On 31 December 19X5 Boycott Ltd's share capital and reserves stood at the following amounts:

	£	£
Authorised share capital		
3,000,000 25p ordinary shares		<u>750,000</u>
Issued and fully paid		
1,440,000 25p ordinary shares		360,000
Reserves		
Share premium account	15,000	
Capital redemption reserve	40,000	
Profit and loss account	<u>55,000</u>	
		<u>110,000</u>
		<u>470,000</u>

On 1 January 19X6 the company made a bonus issue of 1 for 6 25p ordinary shares and on 30 September 19X6 made a rights issue of 1 for 5 25p ordinary shares at 60p each, based on the shares in issue on 1 September 19X6. An interim dividend of 1.5p was paid on 31 July 19X6.

There was a final proposed dividend of 2.5p.

The profit for the financial year after taxation but before dividends was £56,000.

19 What is the total number of shares in issue at 31 December 19X6?

A 1,572,000 shares
B 1,800,000 shares
C 1,986,000 shares
D 2,016,000 shares

Circle your answer

A B C D

20 What is the total dividend for the year?

A £18,925
B £30,000
C £47,600
D £75,600

Circle your answer

A B C D

11: COMPANY ACCOUNTS

21 Given that the capital reserves are used first to cover the bonus issue what is the total balance carried forward on profit and loss account at 31 December 19X6?

A £10,400
B £30,400
C £34,000
D £106,000

Circle your answer

A B C D

22 A company's issued share capital consists of 500,000 ordinary shares of 10p each and 100,000 8% preference shares of £1 each. Profit after tax for 19X6 amounted to £135,000. The directors resolved to transfer £12,000 to a plant replacement reserve and proposed an ordinary dividend of 12% for the year. If retained profits brought forward on 1 January 19X6 were £212,000, calculate the balance of retained profits carried forward at 31 December 19X6.

A £103,000
B £267,000
C £321,000
D £345,000

Circle your answer

A B C D

Data for questions 23 - 25

A company's balance sheets at 31 December 19X6 and 19X7 included the following amounts:

	19X7 £	19X6 £
Fixed assets at net book value	21,866	18,716
Corporation tax payable	760	610
Proposed dividends	420	400
Ordinary shares of 50p each	18,000	16,000
Share premium account	1,000	400
Revaluation reserve	400	-
Retained profits	5,700	3,900

During the year ended 31 December 19X7 the following transactions occurred:

	£
Tax liability for 19X6 finally agreed and paid	630
Dividends paid	400
Proceeds on sale of fixed assets (net book value £370)	580
Purchase of fixed assets	4,220

11: COMPANY ACCOUNTS

23 Calculate the net profit before tax for the year ended 31 December 19X7.

A £1,800
B £2,980
C £3,000
D £3,400

Circle your answer

A   B   C   D

24 What was the company's depreciation charge for 19X7?

A £700
B £730
C £890
D £1,100

Circle your answer

A   B   C   D

25 What was the issue price of the ordinary shares issued during 19X7?

A 50p
B 65p
C 100p
D 130p

Circle your answer

A   B   C   D

26 The 19X7 accounts of the Cowboy Construction Company Ltd include a note describing legal action being taken by a client company. The client is claiming compensation for faulty work carried out by Cowboy during the year. Cowboy disputes the claim and will defend the action in the courts. In the meantime, it has made no provision for eventual payment.

In the accounts of Cowboy, this is an example of:

A a capital commitment
B a post balance sheet event
C a contingent liability
D an accrued charge

Circle your answer

A   B   C   D

CHAPTER 12

FUNDS STATEMENTS

> This chapter covers the following topics:
> - The purpose of a funds statement
> - The four sections of a funds statement
> - The format of a funds statement

1. The purpose of a funds statement

1.1 A statement of source and application of funds (often referred to more briefly as a funds statement) shows the sources from which a business has derived funds and the ways in which the total funds available have been applied.

1.2 On a first reading, this may sound like the purpose of a profit and loss account. But an important distinction is that a funds statement, as its name suggests, is concerned only with transactions that involve an actual flow of funds into or out of the business. The calculation of profit in a profit and loss account is different, because transactions such as the annual depreciation charge are included although they are merely bookkeeping entries and do not involve the movement of funds.

1.3 Another distinction is that *capital* transactions often involve large flows of funds but do not appear in the profit and loss account. This applies both to capital expenditure on fixed assets and capital income from share or debenture issues.

2. The four sections of a funds statement

2.1 Funds statements may be prepared in a variety of formats: there is no definitive regulation on the subject. But whatever the format adopted, the four sections discussed below are likely to appear in the same shape or form.

2.2 *Funds generated from operations.* The starting point for this figure is the profit before tax, but this must be adjusted in respect of any items not involving the movement of funds. The most common example of such items is the annual depreciation charge.

2.3 *Funds from other sources.* Other sources of funds may include share issues, debenture issues, and the proceeds on disposal of fixed assets.

12: FUNDS STATEMENTS

2.4 *Application of funds.* Funds may be applied to pay tax and dividends, to invest in new fixed assets or to redeem share or loan capital.

2.5 *Movements in working capital.* The difference between the total sources of funds in the year and the total applications of funds will be reflected in a change in working capital. This section will be broken down into movements in stocks, debtors, creditors and net liquid funds (ie cash/bank balances and short-term investments).

3. The format of a funds statement

3.1 To avoid ambiguity, the following format and terminology are assumed throughout the questions in this chapter. (The figures are illustrative only.)

STATEMENT OF SOURCE AND APPLICATION OF FUNDS
FOR THE YEAR ENDED 31 DECEMBER 19X6

	£	£
Source of funds		
Profit before taxation		27,800
Adjustment for items not involving the movement of funds:		
eg Depreciation	2,700	
Profit on disposal of fixed assets	1,800	
		900
Total generated from operations		28,700
Other sources of funds:		
eg Proceeds from sale of fixed assets	3,900	
Issue of shares	12,000	
		15,900
Total source of funds		44,600
Application of funds:		
eg Taxation paid	10,200	
Dividends paid	13,600	
Purchase of fixed assets	12,400	
		36,200
		8,400
Movements in working capital		
Increase in stocks	5,600	
Decrease in debtors	(2,200)	
Decrease in creditors	5,800	
	9,200	
Decrease in net liquid funds	800	
		8,400

12: FUNDS STATEMENTS

QUESTIONS

1 In a statement of source and application of funds which one of the items below would *not* appear as an application of funds?

A The nominal value of debentures redeemed at par during the year

B The dividends paid to preference shareholders during the year

C The profit and loss charge for taxation during the year

D The purchase of long-term investments

Circle your answer

A   B   C   D

2 In a statement of source and application of funds, a decrease in loan capital would be shown as:

A a movement in working capital
B a source of funds
C an application of funds
D an adjustment not involving the movement of funds

Circle your answer

A   B   C   D

3 In a statement of source and application of funds which one of the items below might appear as a source of funds?

A Revaluation of fixed assets
B Profit on disposal of fixed assets
C Purchase of fixed assets
D Proceeds on disposal of fixed assets

Circle your answer

A   B   C   D

4 In a statement of source and application of funds which one of the following might be disclosed as a decrease in working capital?

A Increase in current liabilities
B Increase in long-term debentures
C Increase in short-term investments
D Decrease in bank overdraft

Circle your answer

A   B   C   D

12: FUNDS STATEMENTS

5 In a statement of source and application of funds, which one of the following is *not* an 'adjustment for items not involving the movement of funds'?

A Profit on disposal of fixed assets
B Surplus on revaluation of fixed assets
C Amortisation of goodwill
D Depreciation of freehold buildings

Circle your answer

A   B   C   D

6 In a statement of source and application of funds which one of the following would be disclosed as an 'adjustment for items not involving the movement of funds'?

A An increase in the provision for doubtful debts

B The premium on a new share issue

C A discount on the redemption of debentures

D An amount written off deferred development expenditure

Circle your answer

A   B   C   D

7 The profit and loss account of Tammy Ltd shows depreciation for the year of £9,200. During the year, the company received £13,700 on the disposal of assets with an original cost of £22,800 and a net book value of £14,500. The profit before tax for the year is shown in the profit and loss account as £21,600.

In the company's funds statement what amount would be shown as the total generated from operations?

A £11,600
B £13,200
C £30,000
D £31,600

Circle your answer

A   B   C   D

8 The profit and loss account of Thomas Ltd shows a profit before tax of £72,560. During the year the company disposed of assets which had originally cost £18,400 and were 50% depreciated; the proceeds on disposal were £11,500. The profit and loss account also includes a charge of £1,000 in respect of development costs written off.

In the company's funds statement what amount would be shown as the total generated from operations?

12: FUNDS STATEMENTS

    A   £70,260
    B   £71,260
    C   £73,860
    D   £75,860

Circle your answer

A   B   C   D

9 The profit and loss account for 19X7 of Thimble Ltd shows a profit after tax of £61,950. The tax charge based on the year's profits is £15,900 but the tax actually paid during the year is £17,200. Depreciation for the year is £8,500.

In the company's balance sheet at 31 December 19X6, development costs stood at £12,100. During 19X7 the company's development expenditure amounted to £6,400. The total development costs carried forward in the balance sheet at 31 December 19X7 are £14,300.

In the funds statement for 19X7 what amount would be shown as the total generated from operations?

    A   £65,150
    B   £90,550
    C   £91,850
    D   £92,750

Circle your answer

A   B   C   D

10 Trinder Ltd made a profit before tax of £54,300, on which the tax charge was £8,600. The company made a loss of £2,000 on the disposal of a fixed asset which had a net book value of £4,500. This loss, and also depreciation of £3,600, were charged in arriving at the profit before tax. During the year 2,000 £1 ordinary shares were issued at a premium of 100%.

In the company's funds statement what amount would be shown as the total sources of funds?

    A   £55,200
    B   £57,800
    C   £63,900
    D   £66,400

Circle your answer

A   B   C   D

11 The following balances have been extracted from successive balance sheets of Tuppence Ltd.

	Year 1 £	Year 2 £
Issued share capital	21,000	25,000
Share premium account	2,500	5,800
10% debentures, repayable in year 7	18,000	20,000

During year 2 the company disposed of fixed assets with an original cost of £8,200 and a net book value of £2,500. The proceeds on disposal were £7,300.

12: FUNDS STATEMENTS

Given that the total funds generated from operations in year 2 were £23,500, what is the figure for total sources of funds appearing in the year 2 funds statement?

A £35,300
B £36,800
C £37,600
D £40,100

Circle your answer

A   B   C   D

12 The following balances have been extracted from successive balance sheets of Tony plc:

	31 December 19X5 £	31 December 19X6 £
Issued share capital	15,000	25,000
Share premium account	8,000	7,000
10% debentures 19X6-X9	20,000	14,000

During the year a bonus issue of 5,000 shares was made. The issue was financed from the share premium account. Other issues made during the year were for cash.

Given that the total funds generated from operations in 19X6 were £18,600, what is the figure of total sources of funds appearing in the 19X6 funds statement?

A £21,600
B £22,600
C £27,600
D £33,600

Circle your answer

A   B   C   D

13 Timothy Ltd made a profit before tax of £73,400 in the year ended 31 December 19X6, the company's first year of trading. Development costs of £12,000 were incurred during the year and it was decided that half of this amount could be capitalised.

Initial capital had been provided on 1 January 19X6 by an issue of 30,000 50p shares at a premium of 10%. This had enabled the company to purchase a freehold property for £20,000. At the end of the year it was decided to revalue this property to £34,000. No depreciation was charged on the property, but depreciation for the year on other fixed assets amounted to £4,500.

Calculate the total sources of funds appearing in the company's funds statement for 19X6.

A £100,400
B £106,400
C £114,400
D £116,900

Circle your answer

A   B   C   D

12: FUNDS STATEMENTS

Data for questions 14 - 15

The following extracts are taken from the accounts of Teddy Ltd for the year ended 31 December 19X5.

Profit and loss account (extract)

	£	£
Profit before tax		75,400
Taxation		21,800
Profit after tax		53,600
Dividends: paid	4,900	
proposed	9,800	
		14,700
Retained profits		38,900

Balance sheets at 31 December (extracts)

	19X6 £	19X5 £
Corporation tax payable	18,200	16,500
ACT payable	1,900	1,500
Proposed dividends	9,800	7,800

14 What amount would appear in the funds statement for 19X6 in respect of taxation?

- A £19,700
- B £20,100
- C £21,800
- D £23,900

Circle your answer

A   B   C   D

15 What amount would appear in the funds statement for 19X6 in respect of dividends?

- A £4,900
- B £12,700
- C £14,700
- D £16,700

Circle your answer

A   B   C   D

12: FUNDS STATEMENTS

Data for questions 16 - 17

The fixed assets of Toucan Ltd were stated in the balance sheet at 31 December 19X5 at their net book value of £18,500. During 19X6 assets with a net book value of £2,400 were sold, realising a profit of £1,300. The depreciation charge for 19X6 was £5,250. Assets with a net book value of £6,800 were revalued during the year to £15,000. At 31 December 19X6 the company's balance sheet showed the net book value of fixed assets as £51,200.

16 In the company's funds statement for 19X6 what amount will appear under application of funds in respect of fixed assets?

A £30,850
B £32,150
C £40,350
D £48,550

Circle your answer

A   B   C   D

17 Given that the profit before tax for 19X6 was £73,590, what is the figure of total funds generated from operations in 19X6?

A £69,640
B £77,540
C £78,840
D £85,740

Circle your answer

A   B   C   D

Data for questions 18 - 19

Extracts from a company's balance sheets show the following fixed assets at net book value:

	30 June 19X6 £	30 June 19X7 £
Intangible assets		
Development costs	60,000	95,000
Tangible assets		
Freehold	750,000	1,230,000
Plant and machinery	320,000	370,000
Fixtures and fittings	105,000	90,000

Cont...

138

12: FUNDS STATEMENTS

> The expenditure for the year on development projects had been £55,000. The building element of the freehold was depreciated by £6,000 and then revalued on 30 June 19X7 by £95,000. Plant and machinery which had cost £49,000 when purchased in January 19X2 and had an estimated life of 7 years and no residual value was disposed of in November 19X6 for £8,000. Depreciation on the other plant and machinery for the year amounted to £37,000. Fixtures and fittings, of which there were no disposals during the year, are depreciated at the rate of 33⅓ % pa on the reducing balance method.
>
> The company takes account of a full year's depreciation in the year of purchase.

18 What is the total figure included under 'adjustment for items not involving the movement of funds' in respect of fixed assets?

A £84,000
B £90,000
C £92,000
D £114,000

Circle your answer

A   B   C   D

19 What is the total expenditure on tangible and intangible fixed assets included under 'application of funds'?

A £512,000
B £562,000
C £577,000
D £671,000

Circle your answer

A   B   C   D

20 The following balances were extracted from a company's balance sheets at successive year ends:

	Year 1 £	Year 2 £
Stocks	12,000	17,000
Debtors	8,000	7,500
Cash at bank	4,000	-
Bank overdraft	-	3,000
Creditors	10,000	9,000

In the company's funds statement for year 2 the net change in working capital would appear as:

A an increase of £12,500
B a decrease of £500
C a decrease of £1,500
D a decrease of £3,500

Circle your answer

A   B   C   D

12: FUNDS STATEMENTS

21 The following balances were extracted from a company's balance sheets at successive year ends:

	Year 1 £	Year 2 £
Stocks	29,000	18,000
Debtors	18,000	24,000
Cash at bank	-	14,000
Bank overdraft	2,000	-
Proposed dividends	9,000	14,000
Tax payable	15,000	11,000
Other creditors	13,000	9,000

In the company's funds statement for year 2 the net change in working capital would appear as:

A an increase of £15,000
B an increase of £14,000
C an increase of £7,000
D a decrease of £17,000

Circle your answer

A   B   C   D

22 The following balances were extracted from a company's balance sheets at successive year ends:

	Year 1 £	Year 2 £
Long-term investments	26,000	32,000
Short-term investments	19,000	17,000
Other current assets	64,000	52,000
Tax payable	14,000	19,000
Proposed dividends	21,000	15,000
Debenture interest accrued	4,000	7,000
Other creditors	12,000	8,000

In the company's funds statement for year 2 the net change in working capital would appear as:

A a decrease of £13,000
B a decrease of £12,000
C a decrease of £11,000
D a decrease of £7,000

Circle your answer

A   B   C   D

12: FUNDS STATEMENTS

23 The balance sheet of Tubal Ltd at 31 December 19X5 included stocks of £7,800, debtors of £12,900, a bank overdraft of £300 and trade creditors of £6,400. The company's funds statement for 19X5 showed total funds generated from operations £64,300, funds from other sources £28,900 and applications of funds £97,000.

Which one of the following could represent the company's working capital at 1 January 19X5?

A Stocks £5,800, debtors £11,200, cash at bank £2,100, trade creditors £8,900

B Stocks £10,500, debtors £9,400, bank overdraft £200, trade creditors £9,500

C Stocks £4,600, debtors £9,400, cash at bank £1,100, trade creditors £4,900

D Stocks £7,100, debtors £16,100, bank overdraft £1,200, trade creditors £4,200

Circle your answer

A   B   C   D

24 The funds statement of Tunde Ltd for the year ended 31 December 19X5 included the following amounts:

	£
Increase in stocks	11,400
Decrease in debtors	8,900
Decrease in creditors	3,600
Decrease in net liquid funds	12,800
Depreciation	6,900
Total applications of funds	27,500
Funds from sources other than trading operations	7,200

Calculate the company's profit or loss before tax for 19X5.

A £500 loss
B £6,700 profit
C £20,500 profit
D £32,300 profit

Circle your answer

A   B   C   D

25 The funds statement of Tripoli Ltd for the year ended 31 December 19X5 included the following amounts:

	£
Decrease in working capital	13,600
Proceeds on disposal of fixed assets	8,600
Profit on disposal of fixed assets	2,900
Depreciation	12,500
Redemption of debentures	28,000

Calculate the company's profit or loss before tax for 19X5.

12: FUNDS STATEMENTS

A £3,800 loss
B £7,600 profit
C £15,400 profit
D £23,400 profit

Circle your answer

A   B   C   D

26 Tunis Ltd made a profit after tax of £13,600 in the year ended 31 December 19X5. Tax paid in the year amounted to £4,300, although the profit and loss account included a charge of £5,100. Funds from non-trading sources included £8,500 received on the disposal of fixed assets. Applications of funds included £8,000 in respect of a share redemption and there was a net increase in working capital over the year of £14,000.

Calculate the amount by which depreciation for the year exceeded or fell short of the profit on disposal of fixed assets.

A Depreciation exceeded profit on disposal by £900

B Depreciation fell short of profit on disposal by £900

C Depreciation exceeded profit on disposal by £5,200

D Depreciation fell short of profit on disposal by £5,200

Circle your answer

A   B   C   D

CHAPTER 13

ACCOUNTING RATIOS

> This chapter covers the following topics:
> - Why we calculate ratios
> - The main classifications of ratios
> - Some definitions of ratios

1. Why we calculate ratios

1.1 If you were to look at a company's balance sheet or profit and loss account how would you decide whether the company was doing well or badly? Or whether it was financially strong or financially vulnerable? In other words, how would you *interpret* the accounting information provided?

1.2 Interpretation of accounts is a broad subject but in this chapter we are concerned only with one technique of interpretation: ratio analysis. This involves comparing one figure against another to produce a ratio, and assessing whether the ratio indicates a weakness or strength in the company's affairs.

1.3 The key to obtaining meaningful information from ratio analysis is *comparison*. This may involve comparing ratios over time within the same business to establish whether things are improving or declining, and comparing ratios between similar businesses to see whether the company you are analysing is better or worse than average within its specific business sector.

2. The main classifications of ratios

2.1 It may help you to remember the main ratios if they are grouped into categories.

2.2 *Ratios relating to profitability and return*. These include the primary ratio (return on capital employed or ROCE), return on shareholders' capital (ROSC), gross profit percentage and net profit percentage. Remember that ROCE depends partly on the profit margins achieved by a business and partly on the speed at which its assets turn over: high margins and a high turnover rate both improve ROCE.

2.3 *Ratios relating to long-term solvency*. A crucial indicator of solvency is the gearing ratio, which measures the extent to which assets are financed by external sources (borrowing from outsiders) and internal sources (shareholders' funds). Interest cover (the number of times that interest payments are covered by pre-tax profits) is also important.

13: ACCOUNTING RATIOS

2.4 *Ratios relating to short-term solvency and liquidity.* The two key ratios here are the current ratio (current assets ÷ current liabilities) and the quick ratio or acid-test ratio (current assets other than stocks ÷ current liabilities).

2.5 *Ratios relating to asset turnover.* Businesses need to maintain a certain level of working capital to ensure the smooth running of trading operations. But very high levels of stocks and debtors may be a sign of inefficiency. The key indicators are the stock turnover period (the number of days' stock held in store) and the debtors collection period (the average number of days credit taken by credit customers). It is also possible to calculate a creditors payment period, which is the average number of days credit given to the business by its suppliers.

The *cash cycle* is an important concept to remember: it is the time which elapses between the day when a business pays its suppliers for goods and the day when cash is received from customers in respect of those goods.

2.6 *Shareholders investment ratios*

- Earnings per share measures the profits available to equity shareholders, ie the profit after tax and preference dividends, divided by the number of ordinary shares in issue.

- Dividend cover measures the number of times that dividend payments are covered by post-tax profits

- Price earnings ratio (P/E ratio) measures the market value of an ordinary share divided by the earnings per share

- Dividend yield is the dividend paid in a year on any share divided by the market value of the share.

3. Some definitions of ratios

3.1 In practice there may be several valid ways of calculating any particular ratio. Provided that consistency is preserved, comparisons will be meaningful. But you should note that the following definitions are used in the questions in this chapter.

- Gearing = $\dfrac{\text{Prior charge capital (ie borrowings + preference shares)}}{\text{Prior charge capital + shareholders' funds}}$

- ROCE = $\dfrac{\text{Profit before interest and taxation}}{\text{Prior charge capital + shareholders' funds}}$

- ROSC = $\dfrac{\text{Profit after interest and taxation}}{\text{Shareholders' funds}}$

In all these cases, shareholders' funds are taken at book value, not market value.

13: ACCOUNTING RATIOS

QUESTIONS

Data for questions 1 - 7

The extracts below are taken from the balance sheet of Barney Ltd at 31 December 19X3:

	£
Total assets less current liabilities	114,000
Creditors: amounts falling due after more than one year	
10% debentures 19X9	(20,000)
	94,000
Capital and reserves	
Called-up share capital	
Ordinary shares of 25p each	50,000
12% preference shares of £1 each	10,000
Reserves	34,000
	94,000

The company's profit before interest and tax for 19X3 was £37,000. Tax on the year's profits has been estimated as £9,000.

1 Calculate the return on total long-term capital employed earned by Barney Ltd in 19X3.

A 24.6%
B 27.7%
C 32.5%
D 39.4%

Circle your answer

A   B   C   D

2 Calculate the return on shareholders' capital earned by Barney Ltd in 19X3.

A 27.7%
B 29.8%
C 31.0%
D 43.3%

Circle your answer

A   B   C   D

13: ACCOUNTING RATIOS

3 Calculate the return on equity capital earned by Barney Ltd in 19X3.

- A   26.4%
- B   29.5%
- C   31.9%
- D   49.6%

Circle your answer

A   B   C   D

4 Calculate the gearing ratio of Barney Ltd at 31 December 19X3.

- A   17.5%
- B   26.3%
- C   31.9%
- D   50.0%

Circle your answer

A   B   C   D

5 Calculate Barney Ltd's earnings per share for 19X3.

- A   12.4p
- B   13.0p
- C   18.5p
- D   49.6p

Circle your answer

A   B   C   D

6 Calculate the interest cover of Barney Ltd.

- A   11.6 times
- B   13.0 times
- C   17.5 times
- D   18.5 times

Circle your answer

A   B   C   D

7 Calculate the preference dividend cover of Barney Ltd.

- A   20.7 times
- B   21.7 times
- C   29.2 times
- D   30.8 times

Circle your answer

A   B   C   D

13: ACCOUNTING RATIOS

8 Which one of the following formulae correctly expresses the relationship between return on capital employed (ROCE), profit margin (PM) and asset turnover (AT)?

A PM = $\dfrac{AT}{ROCE}$

B ROCE = $\dfrac{PM}{AT}$

C AT = PM × ROCE

D PM = $\dfrac{ROCE}{AT}$

Circle your answer

A B C D

9 Bingo Ltd buys raw materials on six weeks credit, holds them in store for three weeks and then issues them to the production department. The production process takes two weeks on average, and finished goods are held in store for an average of four weeks before being sold. Debtors take five weeks credit on average.

Calculate the length of the cash cycle.

A 5 weeks
B 8 weeks
C 10 weeks
D 20 weeks

Circle your answer

A B C D

10 Which one of the following formulae should ideally be used to calculate the rate of finished goods stock turnover?

A Sales ÷ average stock of finished goods

B Purchases ÷ average stock of finished goods

C Cost of goods sold ÷ average stock of finished goods

D Trade creditors ÷ average stock of finished goods

Circle your answer

A B C D

13: ACCOUNTING RATIOS

11 During a year a business sold stock which had cost £60,000. The stock held at the beginning of the year was £6,000 and at the end of the year £10,000.

What was the annual rate of stock turnover?

A 6 times
B 7 times
C 7.5 times
D 10 times

Circle your answer

A   B   C   D

Data for questions 12 - 17

The trading account of Bruno Ltd for the year ended 30 June 19X6 is set out below:

	£	£
Sales		860,000
Opening stock	100,000	
Purchases	625,000	
	725,000	
Closing stock	76,000	
Cost of sales		649,000
Gross profit		211,000

The following amounts have been extracted from the company's balance sheet at 30 June 19X6.

	£
Trade debtors	120,000
Prepayments	8,000
Cash in hand	12,000
Bank overdraft	16,000
Trade creditors	80,000
Accruals	6,000
Proposed dividends	10,000

In the questions that follow you should assume a year of 365 days. Ignore VAT.

---

12 Calculate the stock turnover period of Bruno Ltd in days.

A 33 days
B 37 days
C 49 days
D 51 days

Circle your answer

A   B   C   D

13: ACCOUNTING RATIOS

13 Calculate the debtors collection period of Bruno Ltd in days.

- A 51 days
- B 54 days
- C 67 days
- D 72 days

Circle your answer

A   B   C   D

14 Calculate the creditors payment period of Bruno Ltd in days.

- A 45 days
- B 47 days
- C 50 days
- D 78 days

Circle your answer

A   B   C   D

15 Calculate the current ratio of Bruno Ltd at 30 June 19X6.

- A 1.25:1
- B 1.93:1
- C 2.04:1
- D 2.12:1

Circle your answer

A   B   C   D

16 Calculate the quick ratio (or acid test ratio) of Bruno Ltd at 30 June 19X6.

- A 1.25:1
- B 1.28:1
- C 1.37:1
- D 1.50:1

Circle your answer

A   B   C   D

17 Calculate the length of Bruno Ltd's cash cycle in days.

- A 2 days
- B 4 days
- C 53 days
- D 100 days

Circle your answer

A   B   C   D

149

13: ACCOUNTING RATIOS

Data for questions 18 - 24

Banjo Ltd made a profit before interest and taxation of £372,000 in the year ended 31 December 19X2. Taxation on the year's profits is estimated at £118,000 and a first and final ordinary dividend for the year of 20p per share is proposed. The company's balance sheet at 31 December 19X2 includes the following amounts:

	£
Total assets less current liabilities	940,000
Creditors: amounts falling due after more than one year	
8% debentures 19X9	(80,000)
	860,000
Capital and reserves	
Called up share capital	
Ordinary shares of 50p each	500,000
7% preference shares of £1 each	200,000
Reserves	160,000
	860,000

The market values of the company's shares at 31 December 19X2 were as follows:

Ordinary shares	220p
Preference shares	160p

18 Calculate the return on long-term capital employed earned by Banjo Ltd in 19X2.

A 27.0%
B 39.6%
C 42.5%
D 43.3%

Circle your answer

A   B   C   D

19 Calculate the return on shareholders' capital earned by Banjo Ltd in 19X2.

A 28.8%
B 35.4%
C 37.5%
D 42.5%

Circle your answer

A   B   C   D

13: ACCOUNTING RATIOS

20 Calculate the return on equity capital earned by Banjo Ltd in 19X2.

- A 27.2%
- B 28.8%
- C 35.4%
- D 46.7%

Circle your answer

A B C D

21 Calculate the gearing ratio of Banjo Ltd at 31 December 19X2.

- A 29.8%
- B 32.6%
- C 40.0%
- D 56.0%

Circle your answer

A B C D

22 Calculate Banjo Ltd's earnings per share for 19X2.

- A 20.6p
- B 23.4p
- C 24.8p
- D 46.8p

Circle your answer

A B C D

23 Calculate the price earnings (P/E) ratio of Banjo Ltd at 31 December 19X2.

- A 2.1
- B 4.3
- C 6.8
- D 9.4

Circle your answer

A B C D

24 Calculate the net dividend yield offered by the ordinary shares of Banjo Ltd. (Ignore taxation.)

- A 4.4%
- B 9.1%
- C 20.0%
- D 40.0%

Circle your answer

A B C D

13: ACCOUNTING RATIOS

Data for questions 25 - 30

The following information has been derived from the accounts of Blighty plc for the year ended 31 December 19X5.

On 31 December 19X5
Current ratio	1.4:1
Quick ratio	0.9:1
Net current assets	£64,000
Ordinary share capital in issue	£300,000
Fixed assets as a percentage of shareholders' funds	90%
Debtors collection period	6 weeks

For the year ended 31 December 19X5
Net profit retained for the year as a percentage of ordinary share capital in issue	40%
Annual rate of stock turnover	8.775 times
Gross profit as a percentage of sales	25%

On 31 December 19X5 there were no current assets other than stock, debtors and bank balances and no liabilities other than ordinary shareholders' funds and current liabilities. Assume a 52 week year.

25 Calculate the amount of Blighty plc's current liabilities on 31 December 19X5.

A £45,714
B £57,600
C £89,600
D £160,000

Circle your answer

A B C D

26 Calculate the amount of Blighty plc's stock at 31 December 19X5.

A £32,000
B £64,000
C £80,000
D £112,000

Circle your answer

A B C D

13: ACCOUNTING RATIOS

27 Calculate Blighty plc's turnover for 19X5.

- A £702,000
- B £875,000
- C £877,500
- D £936,000

Circle your answer

A   B   C   D

28 Calculate Blighty plc's bank balance at 31 December 19X5.

- A £36,000
- B £96,000
- C £108,000
- D £144,000

Circle your answer

A   B   C   D

29 Calculate the total of the overhead expenses appearing in the profit and loss account of Blighty plc for the year ended 31 December 19X5.

- A £114,000
- B £234,000
- C £582,000
- D £816,000

Circle your answer

A   B   C   D

30 Calculate the retained profits brought forward by Blighty plc at 1 January 19X5.

- A £156,000
- B £220,000
- C £340,000
- D £520,000

Circle your answer

A   B   C   D

SECTION 2

MARKING SCHEDULES
AND COMMENTS

1: INTRODUCTION TO ACCOUNTING

MARKING SCHEDULE

Question	Correct answer	Marks for the correct answer	Question	Correct answer	Marks for the correct answer
1	A	1	12	B	(1)
2	D	1	13	D	(2)
3	A	1	14	B	(2)
4	D	(1)	15	D	(1)
5	C	1	16	C	(1)
6	C	1	17	A	(1)
7	B	(1)	18	C	(1)
8	D	(1)	19	C	(1)
9	B	(1)	20	A	(1)
10	C	2	21	B	(1)
11	A	(1)	22	C	1

YOUR MARKS

Total marks available   25   • Your total mark   17

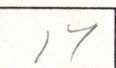

GUIDELINES - If your mark was:

| 0 - 8 | You need to go over this topic thoroughly; then try again. |

| 13 - 18 | Not bad; you have reached a good intermediate standard. There are a few improvements that you could make. Have you identified any regular mistakes you were making? |

| 9 - 12 | Still some weaknesses. Try to identify the places where you are still going wrong. |

| 19 - 25 | Very good. You are well on top of the essential principles in this area. |

157

COMMENTS

Question

1 Strictly, the discussion paper was published by the Accounting Standards Steering Committee, now the Accounting Standards Committee.

4 The fourth concept in SSAP 4 is the accruals concept.

5 Stock would normally be valued at cost, but where realisable value is less than cost prudence requires that the lower value is taken.

6 The accounting equation states that:

Capital + Liabilities = Assets

or

Capital = Assets - Liabilities (= net assets)

Andy's capital is £10,000 and his net assets are therefore also £10,000. *Total* assets are £16,000, but net assets are only £10,000.

7 Closing capital - opening capital = increase (I) in net assets. This means that option B is equivalent to:

$$P = I + D - C_i$$

This is the correct form of the business equation.

8 $I = P + C_i - D$

  $= £(72,500 + 8,000 - 2,200)$

  $= £78,300$

∴ Closing net assets = £(101,700 + 78,300) = £180,000.

Question

9 $I = P + C_i - D$

$= £(35,400 - 6,000 + 10,200)$

$= £39,600$

∴ Opening capital = opening net assets = £(95,100 - 39,600) = £55,500.

10 $I = P - D + C_i$

We are told that C_i is zero, and that (P - D) (ie profit after drawings) is £13,250. Therefore I = £13,250 and closing net assets are £(32,500 + 13,250) = £45,750.

11 $P = I + D - C_i$

$= - £1,800 + £16,300 - £17,700$

$= - £3,200$

12 $P = I + D - C_i$

$= £7,100 + £10,400 - £22,000$

$= - £4,500$

13 ∴ P - I - D (cash) = D (goods) - C_i

£8,500 - £8,200 - £1,800 = - £1,500

14 P - I - D (goods) = D (cash) - C_i

£10,600 -(-£13,700) - £2,800 = + £21,500

15 The cost of freehold premises (including any incidental costs of acquisition, such as solicitors' fees) is a capital item. Depreciation is an annual charge against *revenue;* repairs and decoration are also revenue costs.

COMMENTS

Question

16 A new typewriter would be capitalised as office equipment.

17 Number plates, radio and delivery costs are included in the *capital* cost of acquiring the car. Road tax is an annual charge against *revenue*.

18 Purchase price, carriage and installation are all parts of the *capital* costs of acquiring the machine. The £450 spent on repairs is charged against *revenue*.

19 Leasehold premises are shown under tangible assets; trade investments are shown under fixed asset investments (or possibly current asset investments); preliminary expenses must not be treated as an asset at all.

20 A provision for doubtful debts is disclosed as a deduction from debtors.

21 Carriage inwards is part of the cost of purchasing goods from suppliers; the other expenses relate to selling and distribution and would appear in the profit and loss account.

22 Bad debts are regarded as a selling expense in the profit and loss account, not as part of cost of sales in the trading account. This rules out options A and B. And bad debts recovered are of course good news, not bad, so option C is correct, not option D.

2: LEDGER ACCOUNTING

MARKING SCHEDULE

Question	Correct answer	Marks for the correct answer
1	A	1
2	B	1
3	A	1
4	D	1
5	B	1
6	C	1
7	D	1
8	D	1
9	A	1
10	C	2
11	D	1
12	D	1
13	B	1
14	C	1

Question	Correct answer	Marks for the correct answer
15	C	2
16	B	1
17	D	1
18	A	1
19	D	1
20	A	2
21	A	2
22	C	1
23	A	1
24	C	1
25	B	1
26	A	2
27	B	2
28	B	2

YOUR MARKS

Total marks available: 35   • Your total mark: 27 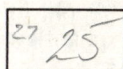 25

GUIDELINES - If your mark was:

0 - 9 You need to go over this topic thoroughly; then try again.

10 - 17 Still some weaknesses. Try to identify the places where you are still going wrong.

18 - 26 Not bad; you have reached a good intermediate standard. There are a few improvements that you could make. Have you identified any regular mistakes you were making?

27 - 35 Very good. You are well on top of the essential principles in this area.

161

COMMENTS

Question

2 Imprest system is a term that describes the process by which a petty cash balance is periodically 'topped up' to a predetermined amount.

3 In the case of a business with no total debtors account in its nominal ledger, the sales ledger would be an integral part of the double entry system. The other records are books of prime entry, which could never be part of the system.

4 The extract records a cash receipt of £140.00 from a credit customer, who is also entitled to a discount of £10.00.

5 The purchase of a fixed asset is recorded by debiting the asset account. Because the purchase is on credit, the credit entry must be in the creditor's account rather than in the bank account.

6 A debit in the bank account represents a *receipt* of cash, presumably because goods have earlier been sold to Smith on credit. Option A is incorrect, because a cash sale (as opposed to a credit sale) would be indicated by the entries: debit bank, credit sales.

7 Because cash leaves the business, there must be a credit to the bank account. The debit would initially be made in the drawings account, though the balance on that account might eventually be transferred to the capital account.

8 Options A and B are ruled out because they relate to rental *income,* which would be a credit (not a debit) in a rent account. Option C is ruled out because there is no entry made in the bank account and therefore no payment can yet have been made.

9 The goods would have been debited to the purchases account when they were originally acquired. Now that they have been removed from the business that debit entry must be reversed by crediting purchases. Since it is the proprietor who has taken the goods the debit must be to his drawings account.

2: LEDGER ACCOUNTING

Question

10 Returns outwards relate to purchases and creditors, and could not affect a debtor's account in any way.

11 When the cheque was originally made out, the entries were: credit bank, debit creditors. These entries must be reversed now that the cheque is being cancelled.

12 Because the cash account is credited, it means that cash (ie notes and coins) has been paid out. Because the bank account is debited, it means that funds have been received in the bank. The entries for the other transactions would be:

   A debit cash, credit bank;
   B debit bank charges, credit bank;
   C debit cash, credit debtors.

13 Returning goods to suppliers means that liabilities are reduced (debit creditors). The credit entry could either be in a returns outwards account or, more directly, in the purchases account.

14 Payments of expenses are credit entries in the petty cash book, and so must be posted to the debit of some other account. This rules out A and B. D is ruled out because a debit in the main cash book would record a receipt of funds into the bank account.

15 The situation in option C is that cash may be received from the debtor (a credit entry in his account) without there being any matching debit entry (because the relevant invoice has not been posted). Options A and B work the opposite way, while option D affects the debtors control account rather than the individual debtor's account.

16 The bill is a liability (a bill payable) in the books of Flintstone. That rules out options C and D. But the liability is *not* in the form of a normal trade creditor (as option A would indicate). It is in the form of a bill of exchange (option B).

17 England Ltd has made a sale (so credit sales account) and created an asset. The asset does not take the form of a normal trade debtor (as option C would indicate); it consists of a bill receivable (option D).

COMMENTS

Question

18 Start plc initially recorded Middle Ltd as an ordinary trade debtor. This trade debtor is now being replaced by an asset in the form of a bill receivable. Options C and D relate to bills payable; while option B refers to the correct accounts, but the wrong way round.

19 The trader discounts the bill for cash. He receives £1,140 (£1,200 less 5% charges), and bank must therefore be debited for this amount. The £60 charges are debited to an expense account. The debtor balance disappears, being replaced by the bill which is now owned by the bank.

20 The bank holds the bill, and will call on Goody to pay its full face value of £4,000 (not just the £3,880 which the bank paid for it). The bank is therefore a creditor for £4,000 and the bad debt must be recognised in full (option A). Option D is wrong because the £120 charges will already have been recognised when the bill was discounted.

21 The ledger account looks like this:

BILLS OF EXCHANGE RECEIVABLE

19X8		£	19X8		£
1.3	Balance b/f	28,500	21.3	Safesure Ltd	6,750
12.3	Dirty Ltd	12,000	31.3	Dirty Ltd	12,000
			31.3	Balance c/f	21,750
		40,500			40,500

22 The cash received from customers includes the basic sales value (100%) plus VAT (15%). The VAT element is therefore

$$15/115 \times £60,720 = £7,920.$$

23 On outputs of £42,780 the business must collect from its customers VAT of £6,417 (15%) to be paid over to Customs and Excise. Against this may be set the £4,554 (15% × £30,360) paid by the business on its inputs. The net amount payable is therefore £1,863.

24 The machinery costs £12,000 plus VAT of £1,800. £13,800 is owed to the supplier (credit creditors £13,800). The machinery is capitalised at its net cost of £12,000; the VAT paid on the purchase is ultimately recoverable from Customs and Excise and is therefore an asset (debit VAT account).

2: LEDGER ACCOUNTING

Question

25 VAT on company cars is *not* recoverable. The cost of the car to the company is therefore its full price inclusive of VAT. This amount must be debited to the asset account and credited to creditors.

26 The company charges VAT to its customers based on net selling prices: £20,000 × 94% × 15% = £2,820. This amount must be handed over to Customs and Excise. It can re-claim £12,000 × 95% × 15% = £1,710. This leaves a net liability of £1,110.

27 The ledger account looks like this:

VAT CONTROL

	£		£
Creditors (purchases)		Balance b/f	2,165
15% × £4,500	675	Debtors (sales)	
Creditors (van)		15% × £5,700	855
15% × £10,460	1,569		
Balance c/f	776		
	3,020		3,020

VAT on entertaining and on company cars is irrecoverable and cannot be debited to the control account.

28 VAT on the company car is irrecoverable. The company's other inputs amount to £(300,000 - 8,000) = £292,000. Of this, the proportion which is recoverable is given by the proportion of taxable sales (£525,000) to total sales (£600,000). Recoverable input tax is therefore £292,000 × 525/600 × 15% = £38,325.

MARKING SCHEDULE

Question	Correct answer	Marks for the correct answer	Question	Correct answer	Marks for the correct answer
1	B	1	15	D	1
2	A	1	16	D	1
3	D	1	17	B	1
4	A	1	18	B	1
5	A	1	19	B	2
6	A	1	20	D	2
7	C	1	21	C	1
8	A	1	22	A	1
9	C	1	23	C	1
10	D	2	24	A	1
11	B	2	25	C	1
12	B	1	26	B	1
13	A	1	27	A	2
14	C	1	28	B	3

YOUR MARKS

Total marks available: 35

• Your total mark:

GUIDELINES - If your mark was:

0 - 9 You need to go over this topic thoroughly; then try again.

10 - 17 Still some weaknesses. Try to identify the places where you are still going wrong.

18 - 26 Not bad; you have reached a good intermediate standard. There are a few improvements that you could make. Have you identified any regular mistakes you were making?

27 - 35 Very good. You are well on top of the essential principles in this area.

COMMENTS

Question

2 The ledger account looks like this:

RENT PAYABLE

19X8		£	19X8		£
31 Dec	Bank - paid in year	1,275	1 Jan	Balance b/f	250
			31 Dec	Balance c/f	
				(prepaid: $\frac{1}{3}$ × £375)	125
				P & L account	900
		1,275			1,275

3 The company should have accrued an amount in respect of the months of November and December 19X4 - $\frac{2}{3}$ × £480 = £320 credit.

4 The bill for the quarter ended 30 November 19X4 had not been paid by 31 December 19X4 but would have been credited to the supplier's account in the purchase ledger. The credit (liability) on the telephone expenses account is just one third of the bill for the quarter ended 28 February 19X5 should have been accrued. The amount is therefore ($\frac{1}{3}$ × £570) = £190.

5 The bill for the quarter ended 31 January 19X6 was paid in 19X5. Only two thirds of this bill (November and December) related to 19X5; the balance ($\frac{1}{3}$ × £810 = £270) is a prepayment at 31 December 19X5.

6 One third of the bill for the quarter ended 28 February 19X6 should be accrued. The amount is therefore ($\frac{1}{3}$ × £720) = £240.

7 The ledger account looks like this:

RENT PAYABLE

19X5		£	19X5		£
31 Dec	Bank - payments in year	3,390	1 Jan	Balance b/f	320
			31 Dec	Balance c/f	270
				P & L account	2,800
		3,390			3,390

168

Question

8

The ledger account looks like this:

TELEPHONE EXPENSES

19X5		£	19X5		£
31 Dec	Bank - payments in year	2,560	1 Jan	Balance b/f	820
	Balance c/f	1,080	31 Dec	P & L account	2,820
		3,640			3,640

9

By classing a liability as an asset the trader has improved his profit figure. He has treated the amount as a £375 increase in profit, instead of a £375 deduction from profit. The net effect is to overstate profit by £750.

10

Rates for 19X8/X9 are £60,720. Rates for 19X7/X8 were therefore £60,720 × 100/110 = £55,200. The profit and loss charge is based on nine months at £60,720 and three months at £55,200, ie:

$$(£60,720 \times \tfrac{9}{12}) + (£55,200 \times \tfrac{3}{12}) = £59,340.$$

11

		£
Rent:	$(£7,200 \times \tfrac{7}{12}) + (£7,800 \times \tfrac{5}{12}) =$	7,450
Rates:	$(£5,400 \times \tfrac{10}{12}) + (£6,000 \times \tfrac{2}{12}) =$	5,500
		£12,950

Alternatively, in ledger account format:

RENT

	£		£
Balance b/f ($\tfrac{1}{12} \times £7,200$)	600	∴ P & L	7,450
Bank (2 × £1,800 + 2 × £1,950)	7,500	Balance c/f ($\tfrac{1}{12} \times £7,800$)	650
	8,100		8,100

RATES

	£		£
Balance b/f ($\tfrac{4}{12} \times £5,400$)	1,800	∴ P & L	5,500
Bank (£2,700 + £3,000)	5,700	Balance c/f ($\tfrac{4}{12} \times £6,000$)	2,000
	7,500		7,500

12

See paragraph 2.5 of this chapter in Section 1 of the book.

Question

13 See paragraph 2.7 of this chapter in Section 1 of the book.

14 The question refers to discounts *allowed by suppliers,* ie discounts received in the books of Arthur. This rules out option D. Options A and B are ruled out because a discount is *not* a receipt of cash; it is a reduction in the amount of cash payable. This only leaves option C: the discounts reduce the amount owed to suppliers (debit creditors) and represent a benefit in the profit and loss account (credit discounts received).

15 Settlement discount is not a trading account item and therefore does not affect gross profit. The effect on *net* profit would be to understate it by £70.

16 Since the debt is now recognised as bad, it must be written out of the debtors ledger (credit debtors). Once the debt is eliminated, the provision should also be removed (debit provision). Option A is wrong because the debit to bad and doubtful debts would already have been made when the provision was first set up.

17 Of the £1,450 balance, 70% (= £1,015) should be written off as bad. Against this should be set the £870 reduction in provision, which is a credit in the profit and loss account. The net effect is a charge against profits of £(1,015 - 870) = £145.

18

	£	£
Bad debts written off		1,500
Less reduction in provision for doubtful debts:		
Provision now required (5% × £124,600)	6,230	
Provision already existing	7,540	
Reduction in provision		1,310
Net charge to P & L account		190

19

	£	£
Bad debt written off - already charged to P & L account when provision was made		-
Bad debt written off		570
Bad debt recovered		(240)
Increase in provision for doubtful debts:		
Provision now required 6% × £(36,800 - 570)	2,174	
Provision already existing	1,460	
Increase in provision		714
Net charge to P & L account		1,044

3: ADJUSTMENTS TO ACCOUNTS

Question

20

	£
Balances per ledger	76,400
Bad debts £(2,300 + 60% × 3,600)	4,460
	71,940
Provision for doubtful debts	
3% × £(76,400 - 5,900)	2,115
	69,825

21 In options A and B the double entry has been preserved, even though not in the correct accounts. In option D the trial balance discrepancy would be £2,000 (£1,000 credited instead of £1,000 debited). In option C the £500 is credited to purchases instead of being debited to fixed assets, and the discrepancy is therefore 2 × £500 = £1,000.

22 Option B: an incorrect amount will be debited to debtors and credited to sales, but the double entry will be preserved.

Option C: no entries have been made, and so the double entry cannot have been disturbed.

Option D: the wrong account has been debited (salaries instead of directors' fees) but the double entry has been preserved.

23 It is incorrect to debit irrecoverable VAT to the VAT account, but it does not breach the rules of double entry and therefore would not cause a TB discrepancy.

24 The sum of £220 should have been debited to drawings and credited to purchases. The reduction in the cost of purchases would have increased gross profit by £220.

25 Item 1 means that both the sales returns account and the debtors account are misstated, but by the same amount. Similarly, item 2 leads to misstatements in both the sales account and the debtors account, but the discrepancies again cancel each other out. In item 3, a cheque for £500 has been debited both to cash and to creditors, without being credited anywhere.

26 Item 1 means that total debits were overstated by £90. Item 2 leads to compensating errors in the purchases and creditors accounts. Item 3 means that total debits were overstated by 2 × £264 = £528.

COMMENTS

Question

27

The suspense account looks like this:

SUSPENSE

	£		£
Wages	300	Rates	440
Creditors	360	∴ Original balance	220
	660		660

28

The suspense account looks like this:

SUSPENSE

	£		£
Accrual	475	Balance b/f	1,508
∴ Asset disposals	1,250	Prepayment	217
	1,725		1,725

Item 3 does not affect the suspense account. In effect the bookkeeper has credited cash and debited sales to keep the double entry intact. The correcting entries would be a debit to drawings and a credit to sales.

172

4: FIXED ASSETS AND DEPRECIATION

MARKING SCHEDULE

Question	Correct answer	Marks for the correct answer	Question	Correct answer	Marks for the correct answer
1	A	1	12	A	1
2	A	1	13	D	2
3	C	1	14	B	2
4	B	1	15	D	1
5	D	1	16	C	1
6	B	1	17	C	1
7	C	1	18	B	2
8	C	1	19	A	1
9	C	1	20	D	1
10	B	1	21	C	1
11	D	2			

YOUR MARKS

Total marks available   25   • Your total mark

GUIDELINES - If your mark was:

0 - 8 You need to go over this topic thoroughly; then try again.

9 - 12 Still some weaknesses. Try to identify the places where you are still going wrong.

13 - 18 Not bad; you have reached a good intermediate standard. There are a few improvements that you could make. Have you identified any regular mistakes you were making?

19 - 25 Very good. You are well on top of the essential principles in this area.

COMMENTS

Question

2 Options B and C are wrong because NBV (despite its name) is not a measure of value. Option D might sometimes be true, but in most cases would not. For example, there may be an estimated residual value which it is not intended to write off; or the reducing balance method may be in use, under which cost is never fully written off.

4 Depreciable amount = £(15,000 - 1,000) = £14,000
Annual depreciation charge = £14,000 ÷ 5 = £2,800
Net book value after one year = £(15,000 - 2,800) = £12,200

5 Depreciation charge in first year = 40% of £15,000 = £6,000
Net book value after one year = £(15,000 - 6,000) = £9,000

6 Net book value after one year (see 5 above) = £9,000
Depreciation in second year = 40% × £9,000 = £3,600

7 Capital cost of asset = £(14,000 + 1,100 + 1,500) = £16,600
Depreciation charge in first year = 10% × £16,600 = £1,660
Net book value after one year = £(16,600 - 1,660)

8 Depreciable amount = £(12,000 - 2,000) = £10,000
Mileage in 19X7 = 21,000
Total expected mileage = 75,000
∴ Charge in 19X7 = 21,000/75,000 × £10,000 = £2,800

9 Depreciation on buildings for three years = 3 × 2% × £55,000 = £3,300
∴ Net book value = £(78,000 - 3,300) = £74,700

10 The cost of the machine is £18,000. Automat has paid £13,000 in cash and has evidently agreed a trade-in value of £5,000 for the old machine. (The asset's NBV is irrelevant.) After one year, the net book value of the new machine is 90% of £18,000 = £16,200.

4: FIXED ASSETS AND DEPRECIATION

Question

11 VAT is not recoverable on company cars. The amount of 15% × £22,000 = £3,300 must therefore be capitalised as part of the cost of the car. At the end of the first year the position is:

	£
Cost £(22,000 + 3,300)	25,300
Depreciation ⅓ × £(25,300 - 10,000)	5,100
	£20,200

12 Take an asset that cost £1,000.

	£
Original cost	1,000
Depreciation in year 1 (20%)	200
Net book value at the end of year 1	800
Depreciation in year 2 (20%)	160
Net book value at the end of year 2	640
Depreciation in year 3 (20%)	128
Still undepreciated at the end of year 3 (51.2% of cost)	512

13

	£
Original depreciable amount	19,000
Less amount already depreciated (²/₅ × £19,000)	7,600
	11,400
Add: further capital expenditure	8,000
fall in residual value	2,700
New depreciable amount	£22,100

(Alternatively:	£	£
Total capital cost £(24,000 + 8,000)		32,000
Less: estimated residual value	2,300	
already depreciated	7,600	
		9,900
		22,100)

14 The new depreciable amount of £22,100 must be written off over the revised remaining life of six years. In each of years 3 to 8 the annual charge is therefore ⅙ × £22,100 or £3,683.

15 No entries in respect of depreciation are made in fixed asset accounts. This rules out options B and C. Option D is correct: the expense account is debited, while the provision is increased by a credit entry. Option A has these entries the wrong way round.

COMMENTS

Question

16

The ledger account looks like this:

MOTOR VANS AT COST

	£		£
Balance b/f	37,300	Disposal account - cost	
Bank	8,500	of vehicle traded-in	12,000
Disposal account - trade-in			
value of old vehicle	5,500	Balance c/f	39,300
	51,300		51,300

17

The ledger account looks like this:

MOTOR VANS ACCUMULATED DEPRECIATION

	£		£
Disposals account		Balance b/f	14,700
(2 × 20% × £12,000)	4,800	Charge for year	
∴ Balance c/f	17,760	(£39,300 × 20%)	7,860
	22,560		22,560

18

The depreciable amount is £(44,000 - 2,000) = £42,000. This is to be written off over seven years (or 84 months). The monthly depreciation charge is therefore £500.

	£
Cost of asset	44,000
Accumulated depreciation (46 months × £500)	23,000
Net book value at date of disposal	21,000
Proceeds on disposal	18,000
Loss on disposal	3,000

19

It is the trade-in value (£12,200 - £7,500 = £4,700) which is relevant, not the net book value. This rules out options C and D. No cash is received by the company; this rules out option B. Option A is correct: the motor cars account is debited, because the trade-in value is part of the cost of the new car; and the disposal account is credited, because the trade-in value represents the amount earned by the company on disposal.

20

The company will include installation costs in the capital cost of the fixed asset, so the asset account must be debited with £77,000. The credits are £70,000 to creditors (the supplier of the asset) and £7,000 to bank (for wages payments).

4: FIXED ASSETS AND DEPRECIATION

Question

21 Option A would lead to a *credit* entry in the asset account. Option B is ruled out because the account is maintained at cost, not at net book value; and anyway, as for option A, the entry would be a credit. Option C is correct: it is the same situation as in question 19 (see explanation there). Option D would only be correct in the unlikely event that the new asset acquired cost exactly the amount of the trade-in value on the old asset.

5: ACCOUNTING FOR STOCKS

MARKING SCHEDULE

Question	Correct answer	Marks for the correct answer	Question	Correct answer	Marks for the correct answer
1	B	1	13	B	1
2	D	1	14	A	1
3	B	1	15	B	2
4	A	1	16	C	1
5	A	1	17	A	1
6	B	1	18	B	1
7	B	1	19	A	1
8	B	1	20	C	1
9	A	1	21	C	2
10	B	2	22	B	2
11	B	2	23	D	2
12	D	1	24	B	1

YOUR MARKS

Total marks available **30**   • Your total mark ☐

GUIDELINES - If your mark was:

0 - 8 You need to go over this topic thoroughly; then try again.

9 - 15 Still some weaknesses. Try to identify the places where you are still going wrong.

16 - 22 Not bad; you have reached a good intermediate standard. There are a few improvements that you could make. Have you identified any regular mistakes you were making?

23 - 30 Very good. You are well on top of the essential principles in this area.

179

COMMENTS

Question

1 No sale has taken place, so it is correct not to have invoiced the customers. But by the same token, the stock still belongs to Justin Ltd and should have been included in the stock valuation at its cost of £1,200.

2 It is correct to exclude free samples from the stock valuation. Applying the basic valuation rule, it is clear that the lower of cost and net realisable value is nil.

3 It is correct to treat the goods as stock at their cost of £7,200. By treating them as sold the company has wrongly taken credit for the profit mark-up of 40/60 × £7,200 or £4,800.

4 The NRV of the stock is £(2,900 - 420) = £2,480. Since NRV is lower than cost, the stock should be valued at £2,480 instead of £2,655. The effect of the error is therefore to overstate profit by £(2,655 - 2,480) = £175.

5 The goods have not been purchased by John Ltd and do not belong to John Ltd. They should be excluded from the stock valuation. By including them at £12,000 the company has overstated profit by that amount.

6 The stock valuation should take account of trade discounts, but not of settlement discounts.

7

	£
Stock at 6 January	74,300
Add back movements out £(1,250 + 140)	1,390
	75,690
Less movements in £(1,155 + 275)	1,430
	74,260

8 Wrong addition has caused stock to be overstated by £(212 - 74) = £138; this amount must be deducted. No adjustment is needed for item 2; valuation at cost is correct since cost is less than NRV. For item 3, it is correct to include goods on sale or return in stock, but the valuation should be cost, not selling price. A reduction of £235 is therefore needed. This gives a final valuation of £(25,850 - 138 - 235) = £25,477.

5: ACCOUNTING FOR STOCKS

Question

9 For each product, take the lower of cost and NRV: £240 + £281 + £157 = £678.

10 The *settlement* discount is irrelevant; the correct cost to use is the list price less *trade* discount. This gives costs of £3,510, £2,828 and £4,095. For product E, NRV at £2,800 is lower than cost. The valuation is therefore £(3,510 + 2,800 + 4,095) = £10,405.

11 In this example, cost includes both direct materials/labour and also production overheads. NRV is expected selling price less expected selling costs.

	Cost £	NRV £	Lower of cost/NRV £
Category 1	4,570	5,320	4,570
Category 2	12,090	11,890	11,890
Category 3	2,300	2,270	2,270
			18,730

12 The effect of each error is to overstate cost of sales and therefore understate profit. The total understatement is therefore £2,900 which means that corrected profit is £(27,200 + 2,900) = £30,100.

13 Returns inwards are a reduction in *sales;* they do not affect cost of sales. Carriage outwards is a distribution expense in the profit and loss account and is therefore irrelevant. The calculation is: opening stock + purchases (including carriage inwards), less closing stock. In other words:

Cost of sales = £(2,850 + 37,640 + 1,840 - 4,270) = £38,060.

14 Cost is £60 per unit. NRV is £(100 - 12 - 8) = £80 per unit. Total balance sheet valuation is therefore £60 × 200 = £12,000.

15 Cost = £(4,720 + 125 + 2,115) = £6,960
NRV = £8,200 × 96% - £845 = £7,027.

COMMENTS

Question

16 Purchases total 141 units, and sales are 100 units. Closing stock is therefore 41 units. On the FIFO basis, the 41 units in stock are taken as the ones most recently purchased. These consist of:

	£
8 units @ £35	280
10 units @ £33	330
<u>23</u> units @ £32	<u>736</u>
<u>41</u>	<u>1,346</u>

17 On the LIFO basis, the 41 units in stock are taken as those purchased earliest. These consist of:

	£
15 units @ £26	390
<u>26</u> units @ £28	<u>728</u>
<u>41</u>	<u>1,118</u>

18 The total cost of all purchases in the six month period is £4,064. On the average cost basis, the 41 units in stock are valued at £4,064 × 41/141 = £1,182.

19 Jones is using the LIFO basis. The issue on 15 January is at the price of the most recent purchase (5 January). Similarly, the issue on 10 February is at the price of the purchase on 8 February. This second issue leaves only 2,000 units in stock from the 8 February purchase. When a further issue of 4,000 units is made on 12 February the cost of the issue is:

	£
2,000 (balance of 8 February purchase) @ £1.75	3,500
<u>2,000</u> (from 20 January purchase) @ £1.72	<u>3,440</u>
<u>4,000</u>	<u>6,940</u>

The unit price of the issue is therefore £6,940/4,000 = £1.735.

20

	Units
Opening stock	3,000
Purchases	<u>90,000</u>
	93,000
Issues	<u>84,000</u>
Closing stock	<u>9,000</u>

5: ACCOUNTING FOR STOCKS

Question

21

Issues	Opening stock	← Purchases →			
		5 Jan	20 Jan	8 Feb	25 Feb
	3,000	20,000	24,000	26,000	20,000
15 Jan		(16,000)			
10 Feb				(24,000)	
12 Feb			(2,000)	(2,000)	
27 Feb			(20,000)		(20,000)
Closing stock	3,000	4,000	2,000	-	-
	@ £1.74	@ £1.68	@ £1.72		
Total	£5,220 +	£6,720 +	£3,440	= £15,380	

22

The normal costs of producing the smaller paper are irrelevant. We have to consider the cost and the NRV of this particular batch of paper. Cost is simply £17,000. NRV is presumably the selling price (£18,000) of the smaller paper, less costs of completion (£500) and costs of selling and distribution (£18,000 × 5% = £900). This means that NRV at £16,600 is lower than the cost of £17,000 and should therefore be taken as the balance sheet value.

23

If prices are rising, the charge to cost of sales will be highest if replacement costs are used. Gross profit will therefore be lowest under this method.

24

The relevant costs are those incurred in getting the goods to their present condition and location. These include costs of conversion and costs of delivery to the customer's premises.

6: CONTROL ACCOUNTS AND BANK RECONCILIATIONS

MARKING SCHEDULE

Question	Correct answer	Marks for the correct answer
1	B	1
2	A	1
3	C	1
4	C	1
5	C	1
6	B	1
7	D	1
8	C	1
9	B	1
10	B	1
11	C	1
12	A	1
13	B	1
14	B	1

Question	Correct answer	Marks for the correct answer
15	D	1
16	D	1
17	B	1
18	C	2
19	B	1
20	C	1
21	D	2
22	D	1
23	D	1
24	C	1
25	D	1
26	D	1
27	A	1
28	B	1

YOUR MARKS

Total marks available: 30   Your total mark: ☐

GUIDELINES - If your mark was:

0 - 8 You need to go over this topic thoroughly; then try again.

9 - 15 Still some weaknesses. Try to identify the places where you are still going wrong.

16 - 22 Not bad; you have reached a good intermediate standard. There are a few improvements that you could make. Have you identified any regular mistakes you were making?

23 - 30 Very good. You are well on top of the essential principles in this area.

COMMENTS

Question

1 The double entry relating to purchase invoices is:

Debit Purchases account
Credit Creditors control account

2 Discounts allowed and returns inwards both reduce the amount owed by debtors, and are credit entries in the control account. Interest charged to customers increases the amount they owe and is a debit entry in the control account. The provision for doubtful debts is an entirely separate ledger account.

3

	£
Amounts due from debtors at 1 January	22,500
Add credit sales in year	107,800
	130,300
Less amounts still unpaid at 31 December	27,300
Amounts paid by debtors in year	£103,000

4

	£	£
Amounts due from debtors at 1 January		21,400
Add credit sales in year		120,100
		141,500
Less: cash received from debtors in year	102,000	
discounts allowed to debtors	8,125	
		110,125
Amounts still unpaid at 31 December		£31,375

5

	£	£
Amounts due to creditors at 1 January (balancing figure)		16,970
Purchases in year		83,200
		100,170
Less: cash paid to creditors in year	79,500	
discounts received	3,750	
contra with debtors control	4,000	
		87,250
Amounts still unpaid at 31 December		£12,920

6: CONTROL ACCOUNTS AND BANK RECONCILIATIONS

Question

6 To record discount received we credit the discount received account. But no cash is actually received from the creditor (we merely reduce any later liabilities to him that may arise). So do not debit bank account (option C); instead debit creditors account (option B).

7 Options A and B lead to the control account and the ledger being mis-stated by the same amount. Option C is wrong because cash *receipts* do not affect the creditors control account. Option D is correct: the total of returns outwards is debited to the control account, but one component of the total has been omitted from the relevant personal account.

8 The ledger account looks like this:

DEBTORS CONTROL ACCOUNT

	£		£
Balance b/f	13,850	Discount allowed	3,940
Sales	121,730	Purchase ledger contras	8,900
		Bank	114,200
		∴ Balance c/f	8,540
	135,580		135,580

Information relating to the provision for doubtful debts is irrelevant, because the provision account is kept completely separate from the debtors control account.

9 Item 1 affects the control account. The daybook total is debited to the control account and in this case the debit is £300 greater than it should have been. To adjust this, reduce the control account balance to £(65,000 - 300) = £64,700. Item 3 also affects the control account. The £1,500 should be a credit entry in the control account, reducing the balance to £63,200.

10 Item 1 affects the control account, but not the individual ledger accounts. The effect of item 2 is to overstate the individual debit balances by 2 x £210 = £420. Item 3 has been correctly recorded in the sales ledger, and can therefore be ignored. (It should also have been entered in the purchase ledger but that does not affect this question.) So the revised total of sales ledger balances is £(63,620 - 420) = £63,200.

COMMENTS

Question

11

The ledger account looks like this:

DEBTORS CONTROL ACCOUNT

	£		£
Balance b/f	21,000	Bills receivable	17,000
Sales	90,000	∴ Bank	79,500
VAT	13,500	Balance c/f	28,000
	£124,500		£124,500

12

The total of sales invoices in the day book is debited to the control account. If the total is understated by £800, the debits in the control account will also be understated by £800. Options B and D would have the opposite effect: *credit* entries in the control account would be understated. Option C would lead to a discrepancy of 2 x £800 = £1,600.

13

Items 1 and 3 affect the total of sales ledger balances; items 2 and 4 are only relevant to the control account.

Item 1 means that the total balances are overstated by £420.

Item 3 means that the total balances are overstated by £560.

The adjusted total is therefore £(83,795 - 420 - 560) = £82,815.

14

Item 2 means that credits in the control account are understated, ie the total debit balance is *overstated*, by £500. Item 4 means that the customer should be re-instated as a debtor to the extent of £804, ie the total debit balance is understated by £804. The adjusted balance is therefore £(82,511 - 500 + 804) = £82,815.

15

The total P & L charge is the cost borne by the employer. This includes gross pay and the employer's own contribution to National Insurance.

16

Employer's NIC is part of the total payroll cost borne by the company and must be charged against profit by debiting to the expense account. The liability to the Inland Revenue is recorded by the credit in the NIC control account. See paragraph 2.2 of the notes to this chapter in Section 1 of the book.

17

This is the situation described in paragraph 2.6 of the notes to this chapter: see Section 1 of the book.

6: CONTROL ACCOUNTS AND BANK RECONCILIATIONS

Question

18 The situation is similar to that of question 17. The business's liability for wages and salaries is reduced (debit control account) because Brian is accepting a reduced cash payment in order to repay the loan. At the same time, the asset 'loan to employee' is being reduced (credit asset account) because the advance is gradually being repaid.

19 The net pay is calculated as follows:

	£	£
Gross pay		54,410
Less deductions:		
PAYE	13,930	
Employees' NIC	4,310	
Savings deductions	1,270	
		19,510
		£34,900

20 The ledger account looks like this:

PAYE CONTROL ACCOUNT

	£		£
Bank	8,920	Balance b/f	22,486
∴ Balance c/f	27,496	Wages and salaries control account	13,930
	£36,416		£36,416

21 The ledger account looks like this:

NIC CONTROL ACCOUNT

	£		£
Bank	8,240	Balance b/f	14,731
∴ Balance c/f	19,551	Wages and salaries control account	4,310
		Wages and salaries expense account	8,750
	£27,791		£27,791

22 A debit balance in the cash book is an asset, ie a favourable balance. Since the bank statement shows an *overdrawn* balance of £210 the discrepancy to be accounted for is £910, not £490. This rules out options A and B. The cash book shows a more favourable position than the bank statement, so option D must be correct: money received has been recorded in the cash book but not yet reflected in the bank statement.

189

COMMENTS

Question

23

	£	£
Balance per cash book		(610)
Items on statement, not in cash book:		
Direct debits	(715)	
Investment income	<u>353</u>	
		<u>(362)</u>
Corrected balance per cash book		(972)
Item in cash book not on statement:		
Customer's cheque		<u>(875)</u>
Balance per bank statement		<u>£(1,847)</u>

24

	£
Balance per cash book	2,125
Unpresented cheques	274
Bank charges	<u>(58)</u>
Balance per bank statement	<u>£2,341</u>

25

The balance sheet figure for cash at bank or bank overdraft is of course the cash book figure, once the cash book is completely up to date.

	£
Balance per bank statement at 31 March	(3,204)
Unpresented cheques	<u>(780)</u>
	(3,984)
Outstanding lodgement	<u>370</u>
Balance per adjusted cash book at 31 March	<u>£(3,614)</u>

The *unadjusted* cash book balance at 31 March would have been £3,568 overdrawn, because we are told that bank charges of £46 were not recorded. Once they *have* been recorded the balance becomes £3,614 as above.

26

This is similar to question 25. The figure we want is the cash book balance, adjusted for bank charges. To derive this, we begin with the balance on the statement, which includes the bank charges, and makes adjustments for the items not yet reflected on the statement: an unpresented cheque and an outstanding lodgement.

	£
Balance per bank statement	(197)
Unpresented cheque	<u>(340)</u>
	(537)
Outstanding lodgement	<u>216</u>
	<u>£(321)</u>

Question

27

	£
Balance per bank statement	167
Outstanding lodgements	<u>643</u>
	810
Unpresented cheques	<u>394</u>
	<u>£416</u>

28

In question 27 we found the balance sheet figure for cash at bank, which represents the original cash book figure as adjusted for the credit transfer of £850 and the overdraft interest of £112. To get back to the original cash book balance we must reverse these adjustments.

	£	£
Cash at bank per balance sheet		416
Adjustment for items not originally appearing in cash book:		
Credit transfer	850	
Overdraft interest	<u>112</u>	
		<u>738</u>
Original (overdrawn) balance per cash book		<u>£(322)</u>

7: INCOMPLETE RECORDS

MARKING SCHEDULE

Question	Correct answer	Marks for the correct answer	Question	Correct answer	Marks for the correct answer
1	A	1	11	B	1
2	C	1	12	C	2
3	B	1	13	B	2
4	B	1	14	C	1
5	A	1	15	B	2
6	D	1	16	A	2
7	A	1	17	B	1
8	A	1	18	C	1
9	B	1	19	A	1
10	D	1	20	B	2

YOUR MARKS

Total marks available: 25   Your total mark: ☐

GUIDELINES - If your mark was:

0 - 8 You need to go over this topic thoroughly; then try again.

13 - 18 Not bad; you have reached a good intermediate standard. There are a few improvements that you could make. Have you identified any regular mistakes you were making?

9 - 12 Still some weaknesses. Try to identify the places where you are still going wrong.

19 - 25 Very good. You are well on top of the essential principles in this area.

COMMENTS

Question

1 Gross profit - expenses = net profit. Therefore gross profit = net profit plus expenses. Option B gives a figure of no particular significance, being the difference between opening and closing stock levels. Option C is wrong because gross profit = sales *minus* cost of goods sold. Option D is the formula for cost of goods sold.

2 This is a reminder of the business equation:

$$I = P + C_i - D$$
$$= £(7,000 + 0 - 9,000)$$
$$= -£2,000$$

In other words, net assets (= capital) have *fallen* over the year by £2,000 and must therefore have been £33,000 to begin with.

3 Harmon's cash purchases for the year are £3,900. His credit purchases are £(27,850 + 720 - 970) = £27,600. Total purchases amount to £(3,900 + 27,600) = £31,500. One way of showing this is to construct a total creditors account.

TOTAL CREDITORS ACCOUNT

	£		£
Cash paid in year:		Balance b/f	970
For cash purchases	3,900	∴ Total purchases	31,500
To credit suppliers	27,850		
Balance c/f	720		
	32,470		32,470

The term "total creditors account" is misleading, because it includes cash purchases as well as credit purchases. Even so, the term is common and the technique is a useful one in incomplete records problems.

4 The cost of sales is £225,000 and gross profit is therefore £75,000. Gross profit as a percentage of cost of sales is:

$$\frac{£75,000}{£225,000} \times 100\% = 33\tfrac{1}{3}\%$$

Question

5 Gross profit is £75,000 and sales are £300,000. Gross profit as a percentage of sales is:

$$\frac{£75,000}{£300,000} \times 100\% = 25\%$$

6 Gross profit percentage is a percentage of sales. In this case gross profit = 20% x £8,000 = £1,600 and therefore cost of sales = £6,400.

7 Gross mark-up is a percentage on cost. In this case, if cost is taken as 100% and the mark-up is therefore 40%, it follows that sales of £70,000 represent 140% of cost of sales. Gross profit is therefore 40/140 x £70,000 = £20,000.

8 The trading account looks like this:

	£	£
Sales		364,800
Opening stock	27,200	
Purchases (314,500 - 570)	<u>313,930</u>	
	341,130	
Closing stock (balancing figure)	<u>37,130</u>	
		<u>304,000</u>
Gross profit (20% of cost, or 16⅔% of sales)		<u>£60,800</u>

9 The trading account looks like this

	£	£
Sales		13,260
Opening stock (balancing figure)	521	
Purchases (10,124 - 243)	<u>9,881</u>	
	10,402	
Closing stock	<u>1,120</u>	
Cost of sales		<u>9,282</u>
Gross profit (= 30% of sales)		<u>£3,978</u>

10 The estimated trading account looks like this:

	£	£
Sales		112,000
Opening stock	18,000	
Purchases (balancing figure)	<u>95,600</u>	
	113,600	
Closing stock	<u>24,000</u>	
Cost of sales		<u>89,600</u>
Gross profit (= 25% on cost, or 20% on sales)		<u>£22,400</u>

COMMENTS

Question

11

Cost of sales = 100/140 x £175,000
= £125,000

Since the stock level is being allowed to fall, it means that purchases will be £13,000 less than £125,000.

12

	Total	Ordinary sales	Private drawings
	£	£	£
Cost of sales	144,000	142,200	1,800
Mark-up:			
12% on cost	216	-	216
20% on sales (= 25% on cost)	35,550	35,550	
Sales	179,766	177,750	2,016

13

	Total	Sales in first three quarters (9/15)	Sales in final quarter (6/15)
	£	£	£
Sales	210,000	126,000	84,000
Mark-up:			
25% on cost (= 20% on sales)	16,800		16,800
20% on cost (= $16\frac{2}{3}$% on sales)	21,000	21,000	
	37,800		

14

Sales = £182,000 ∴ Cost of sales = 60% x £182,000 = £109,200. But cost of sales = opening stock + purchases - expected closing stock, or £(28,520 + 112,900 - x) = £109,200, where x is the value of closing stock *before* the fire. Since x = £32,220, whereas the surviving stock had a cost of only £480, the cost of the stock destroyed must be £31,740.

15

First derive the figure for purchases:

CREDITORS ACCOUNT

	£		£
Bank	133,650	Balance b/f	3,750
Balance c/f	4,900	∴ Purchases	134,800
	138,550		138,550

Next calculate cost of sales: 75% x £174,000 = £130,500. But cost of sales = opening stock + purchases - closing stock, ie £130,500 = £14,300 + £134,800 - closing stock. It follows that closing stock was £18,600.

7: INCOMPLETE RECORDS

Question

16

DEBTORS ACCOUNT				CREDITORS ACCOUNT			
	£		£		£		£
Bal b/f	4,300	Bank	72,500	Bank	46,300	Bal b/f	2,800
∴ Sales	73,700	Bal c/f	5,500	Bal c/f	5,100	∴ Purch's	48,600
	78,000		78,000		51,400		51,400

TRADING ACCOUNT

	£	£
Sales		73,700
Opening stock	6,300	
Purchases	48,600	
	54,900	
Closing stock	2,500	
Cost of sales		52,400
Gross profit		21,300

Gross profit percentage = £21,300/£73,700
= 28.9%

17

	£	£
Cash banked		47,650
Less amounts not derived from sales:		
New capital	220	
Decrease in till balance	50	
		270
		47,380
Add cash received, but not banked:		
Drawings	1,800	
Wages	1,040	
		2,840
Total cash receipts from customers		50,220

In ledger account format:

CASH ACCOUNT

	£		£
Balance b/f	310	Drawings	1,800
Capital	220	Wages	1,040
∴ Sales	50,220	Bank	47,650
		Balance c/f	260
	50,750		50,750

COMMENTS

Question

18

CASH ACCOUNT

	£		£
Balance b/f	175	Expenses	2,150
Sales (100/60 x £35,700)	59,500	Bank	40,100
		∴ Drawings	17,330
		Balance c/f	95
	59,675		59,675

19

We need to calculate credit sales first in order to calculate cash sales.

DEBTORS				CASH			
	£		£		£		£
Bal b/f	2,100	Bank	24,290	Bal b/f	240	Expenses	1,850
∴ Credit				Cash sales		Bank	9,300
sales	23,065	Bal c/f	875	(41,250-23,065)	18,185	∴ Theft	7,275
	25,165		25,165		18,425		18,425

20

DEBTORS				CASH			
	£		£		£		£
Bal b/f	2,150	Bank	37,400	Bal b/f	235	Bank	13,950
∴ Sales	38,450	Bal c/f	3,200	Sales*	21,550	∴ Expenses	7,640
	40,600		40,600			Bal c/f	195
					21,785		21,785

* Total sales = £60,000 (ie 120/100 x £50,000). Since credit sales can be calculated as £38,450, cash sales must equal £21,550.

8: INCOME AND EXPENDITURE ACCOUNTS

MARKING SCHEDULE

Question	Correct answer	Marks for the correct answer
1	D	1
2	B	1
3	B	1
4	B	1
5	B	1
6	A	1
7	B	1
8	A	1
9	A	1
10	A	1
11	D	1

Question	Correct answer	Marks for the correct answer
12	D	1
13	B	1
14	B	1
15	B	2
16	C	2
17	A	2
18	D	1
19	B	2
20	C	1
21	C	1

YOUR MARKS

Total marks available: 25   Your total mark: ____

GUIDELINES - If your mark was:

0 - 8   You need to go over this topic thoroughly; then try again.

9 - 12   Still some weaknesses. Try to identify the places where you are still going wrong.

13 - 18   Not bad; you have reached a good intermediate standard. There are a few improvements that you could make. Have you identified any regular mistakes you were making?

19 - 25   Very good. You are well on top of the essential principles in this area.

COMMENTS

Question

1

	£	£
Subscriptions received in 19X5		790
Less: amounts relating to 19X4	38	
amounts relating to 19X6	80	
		118
Cash received relating to 19X5		672
Add: subs paid in 19X4 relating to 19X5	72	
19X5 subs still to be paid	48	
		120
		792

Alternatively, in ledger account format:

SUBSCRIPTIONS

	£		£
Balance b/f	38	Balance b/f	72
∴ Income and expenditure a/c	792	Cash	790
Balance c/f	80	Balance c/f	48
	910		910

2

	£
Subscriptions received in 19X5	1,024
Less amounts relating to 19X6	58
	966
Add subs paid in 19X4 relating to 19X5	14
	980

Alternatively, in ledger account format:

SUBSCRIPTIONS

	£		£
∴ Income and expenditure a/c	980	Balance b/f	14
Balance c/f	58	Bank	1,024
	1,038		1,038

3

Summary balance sheet at 31 December 19X5

	£
Net assets	
Tables and chairs	380
Playing cards and other accessories	102
Reference books	130
Subscriptions in arrears	27
	639
Subscriptions in advance	80
	559

8: INCOME AND EXPENDITURE ACCOUNTS

Question

3

Funds	£
Accumulated fund	259
Life membership fund	<u>300</u>
	<u>559</u>

4

Accumulated fund

	£
Balance at 31 December 19X5	259
Add back deficit for the year	<u>117</u>
	376
Less transfer from life membership fund	<u>75</u>
Balance at 1 January 19X5	<u>301</u>

5

The trading account looks like this:

	£	£
Sales £(28,340 + 52 × £50)		30,940
Opening stock	3,750	
Purchases	<u>21,200</u>	
	24,950	
Closing stock (balancing figure)	<u>6,386</u>	
Cost of sales (= 60% of sales)		<u>18,564</u>
Gross profit		<u>12,376</u>

6

Gross profit of £12,376 less bar wages of £2,600 = £9,776

7

	£	£
Balance at 1 January		3,780
New enrolments		<u>480</u>
		4,260
Less release to income:		
1 × £80	80	
63 × £5	315	
4 × £6	<u>24</u>	
		<u>419</u>
		<u>3,841</u>

COMMENTS

Question

8

SUBSCRIPTIONS

	£		£
Balance b/f	410	Bank: 19X4	370
		19X5	6,730
∴ I & E account	7,200	19X6	1,180
		19X4 subs written off	40
Balance c/f	1,180	Balance c/f	470
	8,790		8,790

9

CREDITORS

	£		£
Bank	5,685	Bal b/f	435
Bal c/f	363	∴ Purch's	5,613
	6,048		6,048

DEBTORS

	£		£
Bal b/f	12	Bank (6,064 + 1,040)	7,104
∴ Sales	7,100	Bal c/f	8
	7,112		7,112

The trading account shows sales of £7,100 and cost of sales £5,680 (100/125 x £7,100). Since opening stock is £390 and purchases are £5,613, closing stock is £323.

10

Sales are £7,100, cost of sales is £5,680, and so gross profit is £1,420. From this must be deducted barman's wages of £1,040.

11

The club takes credit for subscriptions as soon as they fall due. This means that the subscriptions receivable account is debited with £10,000 on 1 January. (At 31 March a debit balance of £800 will remain on this account in respect of subscriptions due but unpaid.) The credit entries are £2,500 (3/12ths) to subscription income and £7,500 (9/12ths) to subscriptions received in advance.

12

This is similar to question 11. Subscriptions in arrears will be the balance on the subscriptions receivable account: 4 members @ £75 = £300.

13

	£
500 x £75 x 3/12	9,375
500 x £85 x 9/12	31,875
	41,250

Question

14

	£
Members admitted in 19X2 (six surviving at the end of 19X3) - 6 x £96 x 1/3	192
Members admitted in 19X3 (six surviving at the end of 19X3) - 6 x £108 x 1/3	<u>216</u>
	<u>408</u>

15

	£
Members admitted in:	
19X2 - already released to I & E account	-
19X3 - one surviving (1/3 x £108)	36
19X4 - two surviving (1/3 x 2 x £120)	80
19X5 - eight surviving (1/3 x 8 x £132)	<u>352</u>
	<u>468</u>

16

	£
Members admitted in:	
19X2 - one third remaining (1/3 x 3 x £96)	96
19X3 - two thirds remaining (2/3 x 3 x £108)	216
19X4 - all remaining (2 x £120)	<u>240</u>
	<u>552</u>

17

	£
Members admitted in:	
19X2 - already released to I & E account	-
19X3 - already released to I & E account	-
19X4 - one third remaining (1/3 x 2 x £120)	80
19X5 - two thirds remaining (2/3 x 8 x £132)	<u>704</u>
	<u>784</u>

18

	£
Balance at 1 July 19X6	2,050
Add: donation	450
building society interest	120
dividends (10% x £2,000)	<u>200</u>
Balance at 30 June 19X7	<u>2,820</u>

COMMENTS

Question

19

	£
Balance at 1 January 19X5	11,720
Transfer from I & E account	500
Income on fund assets:	
Loan stock interest (12% x £3,000)	360
Dividends on shares (9% x £6,400)	576
Bank deposit interest	94
	13,250

20

Summary balance sheet at 31 December 19X5

	£
Net assets	
Premises	4,200
Furniture and accessories	512
Reference books	175
Subscriptions in arrears	60
Cash at bank	112
	5,059
Subscriptions in advance	144
	4,915
Funds	
Life membership fund	1,200
Special activities fund	800
Accumulated fund	2,915
	4,915

21

Accumulated fund

	£
Balance at 31 December 19X5	2,915
Add back deficit for the year	275
	3,190
Less transfer from life membership fund	220
Balance at 1 January 19X5	2,970

9: MANUFACTURING ACCOUNTS

MARKING SCHEDULE

Question	Correct answer	Marks for the correct answer	Question	Correct answer	Marks for the correct answer
1	B	1	11	B	1
2	C	1	12	C	1
3	A	1	13	D	1
4	A	1	14	B	1
5	A	1	15	A	1
6	B	1	16	C	1
7	D	1	17	C	1
8	D	1	18	B	1
9	A	1	19	C	1
10	B	1	20	C	1

YOUR MARKS

Total marks available: 20   Your total mark: ☐

GUIDELINES - If your mark was:

0 - 5 — You need to go over this topic thoroughly; then try again.

6 - 10 — Still some weaknesses. Try to identify the places where you are still going wrong.

11 - 15 — Not bad; you have reached a good intermediate standard. There are a few improvements that you could make. Have you identified any regular mistakes you were making?

16 - 20 — Very good. You are well on top of the essential principles in this area.

COMMENTS

Question

1 The cost of an extension is capital expenditure, which would be shown as an asset in the balance sheet.

2 Office wages are not a manufacturing cost; they would appear in the profit and loss account, not the manufacturing account. Factory rent and depreciation of machinery are factory overheads; they are included in factory cost of goods produced, but not in prime cost. Prime cost includes only direct materials and direct production wages.

3 Item A is one part of the cost of raw materials. Items B and D are factory overheads. Item C is an expense of selling and distribution.

4 The manufacturing account looks like this:

	£	£
Raw materials		35,800
Direct labour		<u>53,400</u>
Prime cost		89,200
Production overheads		14,800
Opening work in progress	3,600	
Closing work in progress	<u>4,700</u>	
		<u>(1,100)</u>
		<u>102,900</u>

5-7 *Manufacturing account for 19X5*

	£	£
Raw materials:		
Opening stock	12,940	
Purchases	213,680	
Carriage inwards	<u>3,970</u>	
	230,590	
Closing stock	<u>14,550</u>	
		216,040
Direct wages		<u>96,380</u>
Prime cost		312,420
Factory overheads:		
Wages and salaries £(12,490 + 18,330)		30,820
Other factory costs		<u>63,310</u>
	c/f	406,550

9: MANUFACTURING ACCOUNTS

Question

7

		b/f	406,550
Work in progress:			
Opening stock		42,920	
Closing stock		<u>39,610</u>	
			<u>3,310</u>
Factory cost of finished goods produced			409,860
Factory profit (£409,860 x 15/85)			<u>72,328</u>
Transfer price of finished goods produced			<u>482,188</u>

Carriage outwards is a distribution cost which, like salaries paid for administration staff, is shown in the profit and loss account, not the manufacturing account.

8

The transfer price of goods produced is as follows:

	£
Opening stock	57,375
Goods transferred during 19X6 (£780,000 x 1.08)	<u>842,400</u>
	899,775
Closing stock	<u>51,300</u>
	<u>848,475</u>

To this must be added a 20% mark-up: £169,695. The sales figure is therefore £1,018,170.

9

The profit and loss account shows the *movement* in the provision for unrealised profit over the year.

		£
Unrealised profit at start of year	(£57,375 x 8/108)	4,250
Unrealised profit at end of year	(£51,300 x 8/108)	<u>3,800</u>
Credit in profit and loss account		<u>450</u>

10 & 11

	Assembly £	Finishing £	Total £
Manufacturing overhead	(60%) <u>192,000</u>	(40%) <u>128,000</u>	<u>320,000</u>
Apportioned as follows:			
Product Y	(60%) 115,200	(30%) 38,400	153,600
Product Z	(40%) <u>76,800</u>	(70%) <u>89,600</u>	<u>166,400</u>
	<u>192,000</u>	<u>128,000</u>	<u>320,000</u>

COMMENTS

Question

12 & 13 The provision account looks like this:

PROVISION FOR UNREALISED PROFIT

	£		£
Balance c/f 31.12.19X6		Balance b/f 1.1.19X6	
(£5,460 x 5/105)	260	(£4,620 x 5/105)	220
		∴ Charge to P & L a/c	40
	260		260
∴ Credit to P & L a/c	80	Balance b/f 1.1.19X7	260
Balance c/f 31.12.19X7			
(£3,780 x 5/105)	180		
	260		260

14 The mark-up is charged (debited) in the manufacturing account to increase production cost to transfer price. It is credited in the profit and loss account, so that the net effect on reported profits is nil. The purpose of this transfer is to indicate how much profit has been earned by the manufacturing side of the business, and how much by the trading activities.

The provision for unrealised profit is used in a separate exercise to reflect the amount of mark-up tied up in closing stocks.

15

	£
Provision required in 19X8 (£87,975 x 25/125)	17,595
Provision required in 19X7 (£58,650 x 25/125)	11,730
Increase required (charge to P & L account)	5,865

16 Manufacturing stocks include consumable stores, raw materials and work in progress. These are reflected in the manufacturing account. The trading account must also reflect stocks of finished goods and packing materials (delivery cases).

Question

17-19

Manufacturing account for the year ended 31 December 19X5

	£	£
Raw materials:		
Opening stock	22,750	
Purchases	151,500	
Carriage inwards	3,410	
	177,660	
Closing stock	18,630	
		159,030
Direct labour		87,200
Prime cost		246,230
Factory overheads:		
Depreciation of plant		12,900
Other (30% of £(125,800 + 4,200))		39,000
		298,130
Work in progress:		
Opening stock	37,610	
Closing stock	41,260	
		3,650
Factory cost of finished goods produced		294,480
Factory profit (25%)		73,620
Transfer price of finished goods produced		368,100

The cost of one unit of production was £294,480/9,000 = £32.72.

20

The trading account is as follows:

	£
Opening stock (£44,800 x 100/112)	40,000
Factory cost of finished goods produced	638,400
	678,400
Closing stock (£50,400 x 100/112)	45,000
Cost of goods sold	633,400
Mark-up (25%)	158,350
∴ Sales	791,750

10: PARTNERSHIP ACCOUNTS

MARKING SCHEDULE

Question	Correct answer	Marks for the correct answer	Question	Correct answer	Marks for the correct answer
1	C	1	14	B	2
2	A	1	15	B	1
3	D	1	16	B	1
4	A	1	17	D	1
5	B	1	18	A	1
6	D	1	19	A	1
7	A	1	20	B	2
8	A	1	21	B	2
9	C	1	22	A	1
10	C	1	23	A	1
11	B	2	24	B	1
12	B	2	25	A	2
13	C	2	26	D	1

YOUR MARKS

Total marks available: 33   Your total mark: ☐

GUIDELINES - If your mark was:

0 - 10 You need to go over this topic thoroughly; then try again.

11 - 16 Still some weaknesses. Try to identify the places where you are still going wrong.

17 - 25 Not bad; you have reached a good intermediate standard. There are a few improvements that you could make. Have you identified any regular mistakes you were making?

26 - 33 Very good. You are well on top of the essential principles in this area.

211

COMMENTS

Question

1

The corrected account looks like this:

CURRENT ACCOUNT

	£		£
Drawings	6,200	Balance b/f	270
Balance c/f	7,070	Interest on capital	2,800
		Salary	1,500
		Net profit	8,700
	13,270		13,270

4

The petrol bills have been debited to motor vehicle expenses. This is incorrect and should be revised (so credit motor vehicle expenses). Because they are private expenses of the partner they should be debited to his drawings account.

5

Interest on partners' capital is an appropriation of profit (debit appropriation account). Since partners have earned the money by their investment in the business, their current accounts should be credited with it. (Option D would be theoretically possible, but most firms maintain current accounts separately from capital accounts in order to record such items.)

6

Interest payable by partners increases the amount of profits available for appropriation (credit appropriation account). It must be charged against the partners (debit partners' current accounts).

8 & 9

The appropriations earned by each partner are as follows:

	Faith £	Hope £	Charity £	Total £
Interest on capital	1,600	1,200	960	3,760
Salary		8,000		8,000
	1,600	9,200	960	11,760
Residual profit (3:2:1)	36,120	24,080	12,040	72,240
	37,720	33,280	13,000	84,000

10: PARTNERSHIP ACCOUNTS

Question

10

	£
Net profit from trading	32,000
Add interest on drawings (10% x £(12,000 + 15,000))	2,700
	34,700
Less interest on capital (6% x £(8,000 + 6,000))	840
Residual profit	33,860

11

	£
Interest on capital (6% x £8,000)	480
Share of residual profit (3/5 x £33,860)	20,316
	20,796
Less interest on drawings (10% x £12,000)	1,200
Net transfers from appropriation account	19,596

12

	£
Net profit before loan interest	38,700
Interest on drawings* 10% x £(4,300 + 4,600 + 4,000)	1,290
	39,990
Less interest on loan (5%)	1,000
Residual profits	38,990
Alpha's share (two fifths)	£15,596

* Based on the average amount of drawings during the year.

13

The appropriations earned by each partner are as follows:

	Nakert £	Wheezy £	Faggs £	Total £
Salary	6,000	6,000	5,000	17,000
Less interest on drawings	180	192	150	522
	5,820	5,808	4,850	16,478
Residual loss (3:5:2)	743	1,239	496	2,478
	5,077	4,569	4,354	14,000

213

COMMENTS

Question

14
Appropriation account for 19X8

	Nobby £	Fingers £	Swag £	Total £
Net profit				30,000
Interest on drawings	(320)	(240)	(240)	800
				30,800
Salaries		7,000	4,800	11,800
Residual profit (2:5:3)	3,800	9,500	5,700	19,000
Net transfer to current accounts	3,480	16,260	10,260	

15
Fingers's capital account

	£
Opening balance	12,000
Net transfer from appropriation account (see above)	16,260
	28,260
Less drawings	3,000
Closing balance	25,260

16
Amount due to Forsyze

	£
Capital account	21,000
Current account	(1,400)
Share of goodwill (£8,000 × 2/5)	3,200
Share of revaluation surplus (£3,000 × 2/5)	1,200
	24,000

17

MAYNE'S LOAN ACCOUNT

	£		£
Car	4,800	Capital account	15,000
Balance: loan account	22,600	Current account	7,300
		Share of goodwill	3,600
		Share of revaluation	1,500
	27,400		27,400

10: PARTNERSHIP ACCOUNTS

Question

18

PARTNERS' CAPITAL ACCOUNTS

		Luck £	Flaw £	Reagan £			Luck £	Flaw £	Reagan £
30.6.X6	Goodwill	1,600	1,600	1,600	1.1.X6	Bank	8,000	8,000	
	Bal c/f	10,300	10,300	8,400	30.6.X6	P&L	1,500	1,500	
						Bank			10,000
						Goodwill	2,400	2,400	
		11,900	11,900	10,000			11,900	11,900	10,000

19

PARTNERS' CAPITAL ACCOUNTS

	Bass £	Guinness £	Diamond £	Mackeson £
Credits				
Balance b/f	18,000	10,000	6,000	
Bank				10,000
Goodwill (3:2:1)	6,000	4,000	2,000	
	24,000	14,000	8,000	10,000
Debits				
Goodwill (2:2:1:1)	(4,000)	(4,000)	(2,000)	(2,000)
	20,000	10,000	6,000	8,000

20 - 23

Appropriation account for 19X5

	1.1.X5- 30.6.X5 £	1.7.X5- 31.12.X5 £		1.1.X5- 30.6.X5 £	1.7.X5- 31.12.X5 £
First 6 months			Net profit	26,000	36,000
Share of profit:					
Grub	19,500				
Grime	6,500				
Last 6 months					
Loan interest					
10% × £44,250 × 6/12 *		2,212			
Share of profit:					
Grime		20,273			
Scrub		13,515			
	26,000	36,000		26,000	36,000

* See below for calculation of loan a/c balance.

COMMENTS

Question

PARTNERS' CAPITAL ACCOUNTS

		Grub £	Grime £			Grub £	Grime £
30.6.X5	Bank	20,000		1.1.X5	Balance b/f	38,000	29,000
	Loan a/c	44,250		30.6.X5	Approp. a/c	19,500	6,500
	Balance c/d		37,750		Goodwill	6,750	2,250
		64,250	37,750			64,250	37,750

		Grime £	Scrub £			Grime £	Scrub £
1.7.X5	Goodwill	5,400	3,600	1.7.X5	Balance b/d	37,750	
					Bank		12,000
31.12.X5	Balance c/f	52,623	21,915	31.12.X5	Approp. a/c	20,273	13,515
		58,023	25,515			58,023	25,515

24 & 25

Alpha and Beta: capital accounts

	Alpha £	Beta £		Alpha £	Beta £
Bank		10,000	Balances b/f	5,000	3,000
Balance c/f	12,000		Revaluation	2,000	2,000
			Goodwill	5,000	5,000
	12,000	10,000		12,000	10,000

Alpha, Gamma and Delta: capital accounts

	Alpha £	Gamma £	Delta £		Alpha £	Gamma £	Delta £
Devaluation		3,000	3,000	Balances b/f		6,000	2,000
Goodwill	6,000	6,000	6,000	Transfer	12,000		
Balances c/f	6,000	1,000		Goodwill		4,000	4,000
				Balance c/f			3,000
	12,000	10,000	9,000		12,000	10,000	9,000

The net tangible assets in the new firm are equal to the new partners' capital balances: £6,000 + £1,000 - £3,000 = £4,000.

26

The asset is revalued (debit asset account) and the surplus is credited to the partners in their profit sharing ratio.

11: COMPANY ACCOUNTS

MARKING SCHEDULE

Question	Correct answer	Marks for the correct answer	Question	Correct answer	Marks for the correct answer
1	C	1	14	A	1
2	A	1	15	A	1
3	B	1	16	A	1
4	D	1	17	C	1
5	B	1	18	B	1
6	D	1	19	D	1
7	A	1	20	D	1
8	C	1	21	B	2
9	A	1	22	C	2
10	B	1	23	C	2
11	A	1	24	D	2
12	B	1	25	B	1
13	D	1	26	C	1

YOUR MARKS

Total marks available **30**   Your total mark ☐

GUIDELINES - If your mark was:

0 - 8 You need to go over this topic thoroughly; then try again.

9 - 15 Still some weaknesses. Try to identify the places where you are still going wrong.

16 - 22 Not bad; you have reached a good intermediate standard. There are a few improvements that you could make. Have you identified any regular mistakes you were making?

23 - 30 Very good. You are well on top of the essential principles in this area.

217

COMMENTS

Question	Comments
1	A company can enter into trading obligations without limit. Its own liability to meet those obligations from its own assets is unlimited. However, if its own assets are insufficient, shareholders will not in general be called on to make up the deficiency; their personal liability is limited.
2	Option B is the company's *issued* share capital; option C is the company's *paid-up* share capital. Option D refers to *borrowings* rather than to share capital.
3	Companies are required to maintain a register of charges on company assets, but not of debenture holders.
4	A company's share capital increases when it issues shares to someone. Once the shares have been issued, any transfer from one person to another has no effect on the company's share capital.
5	Equity capital consists of equity (or ordinary) shares, plus all reserves. Preference shareholders do not participate in the equity of a company.
6	Options A, B and C are three of the specific purposes for which company law allows the share premium account to be used. Only in exceptional circumstances can the account be used to finance the premium on redemption of shares.
7	A capital redemption reserve has the same status as share capital in that it may not normally be reduced without court sanction. However, it is permissible to convert the reserve into share capital by using it to finance an issue of fully paid bonus shares.
8	Debenture interest is paid to debenture holders, who are creditors of the company and do not share in its ownership. Such interest is therefore a charge against revenue in arriving at the profit figure; it is *not* an appropriation of profit.

11: COMPANY ACCOUNTS

Question

9 Dividends are paid in respect of *issued* shares only. Here there are 500,000 shares in issue and the dividend payable is 2p per share. The total amount is therefore 500,000 × 2p = £10,000.

10 The balance sheet figure for share capital (£2,000,000) represents the nominal value of shares in issue. Since the shares have a nominal value of 50p each, this means that there are 4,000,000 shares qualifying for a 3p dividend. The total payable is therefore 4,000,000 × 3p = £120,000.

11 Once again, *authorised* capital is irrelevant. The nominal value of *issued* share capital is 200,000 × 25p = £50,000. The 10% dividend is a proportion of this nominal value: 10% × £50,000 = £5,000.

12 The nominal value of issued share capital is £200,000. A dividend of 20% amounts to £200,000 × 20% = £40,000.

13 Issued share capital consists of 800,000 shares with a nominal value of £80,000. £40,000 represents either a dividend of 50% (not given as an option) or a dividend of 5p per share (option D).

14 £45,000 represents 3% of the nominal value of the company's share capital. The full nominal value must therefore be £45,000 × 100/3 = £1,500,000.

15 The nominal value of the issued shares is simply 40,000 × 20p = £8,000.

16

	£	£
Net profit		184,000
Less dividends:		
Ordinary (200,000 × 5p)	10,000	
Preference (8% × £50,000)	4,000	
		14,000
Retained profit		170,000

Since the directors wish to pay an ordinary dividend, they are obliged to pay the preference dividend also.

219

COMMENTS

Question

17

	Number of shares
Shares in issue at 31 December 19X6 (£600,000 ÷ 25p)	2,400,000
Bonus issue (2,400,000 x 2/5)	960,000
Shares in issue at 31 December 19X7	3,360,000

18

Share capital

	Number	£
Balance at 31 December 19X4	480,000	240,000
Bonus issue	120,000	60,000
Issue for cash (42,000 ÷ 70p)	60,000	30,000
Balance at 31 December 19X5	660,000	330,000

19

Share capital

	Number	£
Balance at 31 December 19X5	1,440,000	360,000
Bonus issue 1 January 19X6	240,000	60,000
Balance at 1 September 19X6	1,680,000	420,000
Rights issue 30 September 19X6	336,000	84,000
Balance at 31 December 19X6	2,016,000	504,000

20

Dividends

	£
Interim paid 31 July 19X6 (1,680,000 shares @ 1.5p)	25,200
Final proposed at 31 December 19X6 (2,016,000 shares @ 2.5p)	50,400
	75,600

21

Profit and loss account

	£	£
Balance at 31 December 19X5		55,000
Bonus issue 1 January 19X6:		
Nominal value of shares issued	60,000	
Amounts financed from capital reserves		
£(15,000 + 40,000)	55,000	
Balance financed from P & L account		5,000
		50,000
Profit after tax for 19X6		56,000
		106,000
Dividends		75,600
Balance at 31 December 19X6		30,400

11: COMPANY ACCOUNTS

Question

22

Profit and loss appropriation account for 19X6

	£	£
Profit after tax		135,000
Dividends:		
Ordinary (12% x £50,000)	6,000	
Preference (8% x £100,000)	8,000	
	14,000	
Transfer to plant replacement reserve	12,000	
		26,000
Retained profit for the year		109,000
Retained profits brought forward		212,000
Retained profits carried forward		321,000

23

The best approach is to reconstruct the profit and loss account for 19X7, inserting the profit before tax as a balancing figure

Profit and loss account for the year ended 31 December 19X7

	£	£
Profit before tax (balancing figure)		3,000
Taxation		
For 19X7	760	
Under-provision for 19X6 £(630 - 610)	20	
		780
Profit after tax		2,220
Dividends		420
Retained profit for the year		1,800
Retained profits brought forward		3,900
Retained profits carried forward		5,700

24

Don't worry if you found this question difficult. It introduces some of the principles you will be practising in the next chapter (on funds statements).

Movements on fixed assets (all figures at net book value)

	£
Balance at 31 December 19X6	18,716
Add: purchases in year	4,220
surplus on revaluation	400
	23,336
Less disposals in year	370
Balance at 31 December 19X7 (before depreciation)	22,966
Depreciation (balancing figure)	1,100
Balance at 31 December 19X7 per balance sheet	21,866

COMMENTS

Question

25 The nominal value of the company's issued share capital increased by £2,000 over the year (from £16,000 to £18,000). This means that 4,000 shares of 50p each were issued. The proceeds of the issue included a share premium of £600 (because the balance on share premium account rose from £400 to £1,000). Total proceeds were therefore £2,600 representing an issue price of £2,600/4,000 = 65p per share.

26 Cowboy may find that it is liable to pay compensation to the client, but this is contingent (dependent) upon the findings of the court. It is not a capital commitment (a sum contracted for, or at least authorised, in respect of an investment by the company in new assets). It is not a post balance sheet event, because the matter has come to light *before* the balance sheet date. It is not an accrued charge (a cost which is known to have been incurred, but for which no invoice has been received).

12: FUNDS STATEMENTS

MARKING SCHEDULE

Question	Correct answer	Marks for the correct answer	Question	Correct answer	Marks for the correct answer
1	C	1	14	A	1
2	C	1	15	B	1
3	D	1	16	B	1
4	A	1	17	B	1
5	B	1	18	D	3
6	D	1	19	C	2
7	D	1	20	C	1
8	B	1	21	A	1
9	B	2	22	A	1
10	D	1	23	D	1
11	D	1	24	B	1
12	C	1	25	A	1
13	A	1	26	B	1

YOUR MARKS

Total marks available 30   Your total mark ☐

GUIDELINES - If your mark was:

0 - 8 You need to go over this topic thoroughly; then try again.

9 - 15 Still some weaknesses. Try to identify the places where you are still going wrong.

16 - 22 Not bad; you have reached a good intermediate standard. There are a few improvements that you could make. Have you identified any regular mistakes you were making?

23 - 30 Very good. You are well on top of the essential principles in this area.

223

COMMENTS

Question

1 Options A, B and D are all common examples of applications of funds. Option C is not: tax actually *paid* in a year would appear as an application of funds for that year, but the profit and loss *charge* for taxation is not the same as tax paid.

2 If loan capital decreases, it is presumably because a repayment has been made. This would mean that funds have left the business and would be shown as an application of funds.

3 The revaluation of fixed assets (option A) is an adjustment to their book values; it does not provide any funds. Option C is wrong because the purchase of fixed assets is an *application* of funds. However, a disposal of fixed assets does lead to an inflow of funds, and it is the proceeds on disposal (option D) which would appear as a source of funds. Any profit on disposal (option B) is again only a book entry: it is the difference between disposal proceeds and net book value.

4 A decrease in working capital means either a decrease in current assets (so option C is wrong) or an increase in current liabilities (so option D is wrong). Long-term debentures, being a non-current liability, are not part of working capital at all: any increase would be shown as a source of funds.

5 A funds statement usually begins with the figure of profit before tax. This figure must be adjusted for any items included in it that do not represent a flow of funds. Options A, C and D are three examples of amounts which are taken into account in arriving at the profit figure, but do not represent movements of funds and must therefore be adjusted for. Option B does not represent a movement of funds either, but it would not be accounted for by adjusting the profit figure because a revaluation surplus would not have been included in the calculation of profit to begin with. It is a movement on reserves which would not appear anywhere in a funds statement.

6 The premium on a share issue and the discount on redemption of debentures affect the amounts received/paid by the business. In other words, they *do* involve the movement of funds. The provision for doubtful debts is a deduction from debtors, and movements in debtors balances are included in the section of the funds statement which shows changes in working capital.

12: FUNDS STATEMENTS

Question

7

Total generated from operations

	£	£
Profit before tax		21,600
Adjustment for items not involving the movement of funds*:		
Depreciation	9,200	
Loss on disposal £(14,500 - 13,700)	800	
		10,000
		31,600

* Both of these items will have been *deducted* in arriving at the figure of profit before tax. They must be added back to derive the total generated from operations.

8

Total generated from operations

	£	£
Profit before tax		72,560
Adjustment for items not involving the movement of funds:		
Take out profit on disposal £(11,500 - 9,200)	(2,300)	
Add back amortisation of development costs	1,000	
		(1,300)
		71,260

9

Total generated from operations

	£
Profit after tax	61,950
Tax charge for the year	15,900
Profit before tax	77,850
Add back:	
Depreciation	8,500
Amortisation of development costs*	4,200
	90,550

DEVELOPMENT COSTS

	£		£
Balance b/f	12,100	∴ P & L charge	4,200
Bank	6,400	Balance c/f	14,300
	18,500		18,500

225

COMMENTS

Question

10

Source of funds

	£
Profit before tax	54,300
Add back: depreciation	3,600
loss on disposal	2,000
Total generated from operations	59,900
Share issue (2,000 x £2)	4,000
Proceeds on disposal	2,500
Total source of funds	66,400

11

Source of funds

	£
Total generated from operations	23,500
Share issue £(4,000 + 3,300)	7,300
Debenture issue	2,000
Proceeds on disposal of fixed assets	7,300
Total sources of funds	40,100

It is necessary to assume that the debentures were issued at par.

12

Source of funds

	£
Total generated from operations	18,600
Share issue - 5,000 shares issued for cash:	
Nominal value	5,000
Share premium (£7,000 - £(8,000 - 5,000))	4,000
Total source of funds	27,600

The bonus issue is not a source of funds and does not appear in the funds statement. It does, however, have the effect of reducing the balance on share premium account from £8,000 to £3,000. Since it has risen back to £7,000 by 31 December 19X6 the premium on the issue for cash must have been £4,000. The debentures are irrelevant in this question: a redemption has taken place and this is an *application* of funds, not a *source*.

13

Source of funds

	£
Profit before tax	73,400
Add back: depreciation	4,500
amortisation of development costs	6,000
Total generated from operations	83,900
Share issue (30,000 x 50p x 1.1)	16,500
Total source of funds	100,400

Question

14 & 15

Application of funds

	Tax £	Dividends £
Liabilities b/f at 1 January 19X6	18,000	7,800
Add P & L charge for the year	21,800	14,700
	39,800	22,500
Liabilities c/f at 31 December 19X6	20,100	9,800
Difference = amounts paid in year	19,700	12,700

16

FIXED ASSETS AT NBV

	£		£
Balance b/f	18,500	Disposal	2,400
Revaluation	8,200	Depreciation	5,250
∴ Purchases	32,150	Balance c/f	51,200
	58,850		58,850

17

Funds generated from operations

	£	£
Profit before tax		73,590
Adjustment for items not involving the movement of funds:		
Depreciation	5,250	
Profit on disposal	(1,300)	
		3,950
Total generated from operations		77,540

18

	£	£
Amortisation of development costs (£60,000 + 55,000 - 95,000)		20,000
Depreciation on freehold		6,000
Loss on disposal of plant:		
Original cost	49,000	
Depreciation in 19X2,19X3,19X4,19X5,19X6	35,000	
Net book value at date of disposal	14,000	
Proceeds on disposal	8,000	
Loss on disposal		6,000
Depreciation on plant		37,000
Depreciation on fixtures and fittings*		45,000
		114,000

* The net book value *after* depreciation (£90,000) is two thirds of the net book value *before* depreciation. Fixtures and fittings must therefore have had a net book value before depreciation of £135,000, being £105,000 brought forward and presumably £30,000 of purchases in the year.

COMMENTS

Question

19

Expenditure on fixed assets

	£
Development costs	55,000
Freehold (note 1)	391,000
Plant and machinery (note 2)	101,000
Fixtures and fittings (see solution to 18 above)	30,000
	577,000

Note 1   FREEHOLD AT NBV *

	£		£
Balance b/f	750,000	Depreciation	6,000
Revaluation	95,000	Balance c/f	1,230,000
∴ Purchases	391,000		
	1,236,000		1,236,000

Note 2   PLANT AND MACHINERY AT NBV

	£		£
Balance b/f	320,000	Disposal	14,000
∴ Purchases	101,000	Depreciation	37,000
		Balance c/f	370,000
	421,000		421,000

20

Movement in working capital

	£
Increase in stocks	5,000
Decrease in debtors	(500)
Decrease in cash at bank	(4,000)
Increase in bank overdraft	(3,000)
Decrease in creditors	1,000
Net decrease	(1,500)

21

Movement in working capital

	£
Decrease in stocks	(11,000)
Increase in debtors	6,000
Increase in cash at bank	14,000
Decrease in bank overdraft	2,000
Decrease in other creditors	4,000
Net increase	15,000

Dividends and tax are treated elsewhere in the funds statement; they do not appear amongst the movements in working capital.

12: FUNDS STATEMENTS

Question

22 Movement in working capital

	£
Decrease in short-term investments	(2,000)
Decrease in other current assets	(12,000)
Increase in debenture interest accrued	(3,000)
Decrease in other creditors	4,000
Net decrease	(13,000)

Short-term investments count as working capital, but long-term investments are fixed assets. Debenture interest accrued is treated like trade creditors.

23 Summary funds statement for 19X5

	£
Total generated from operations	64,300
Funds from other sources	28,900
Total source of funds	93,200
Application of funds	97,000
Net decrease in working capital	(3,800)

The movements in working capital under each of options A to D are as follows:

	A £	B £	C £	D £
Stocks	2,000	(2,700)	3,200	700
Debtors	1,700	3,500	3,500	(3,200)
Cash at bank	(2,100)	-	(1,100)	-
Bank overdraft	(300)	(100)	(300)	900
Trade creditors	2,500	3,100	(1,500)	(2,200)
Increase/(decrease) over year	3,800	3,800	3,800	(3,800)

24 Summary funds statement for 19X5

	£
Profit before tax (balancing figure)	6,700
Depreciation	6,900
Total generated from operations	13,600
Funds from other sources	7,200
Total source of funds	20,800
Application of funds	27,500
Net decrease in working capital	(6,700)
Increase in stocks	11,400
Decrease in debtors	(8,900)
Decrease in creditors	3,600
Decrease in net liquid funds	(12,800)
Net decrease in working capital	(6,700)

COMMENTS

Question

25
Summary funds statement for 19X5

	£
Loss before taxation (balancing figure)	(3,800)
Depreciation	12,500
Profit on disposal of fixed assets	(2,900)
Total generated from operations	5,800
Proceeds on disposal of fixed assets	8,600
Total source of funds	14,400
Redemption of debentures	28,000
Decrease in working capital	(13,600)

26
Summary funds statement for 19X5

	£
Profit before tax (£13,600 + £5,100)	18,700
Excess of profit on disposal over depreciation	900
Total generated from operations	17,800
Proceeds on disposal of fixed assets	8,500
Total source of funds	26,300
Tax paid	(4,300)
Redemption of shares	(8,000)
Increase in working capital	14,000

13: ACCOUNTING RATIOS

MARKING SCHEDULE

Question	Correct answer	Marks for the correct answer	Question	Correct answer	Marks for the correct answer
1	C	1	16	A	1
2	A	1	17	C	1
3	B	1	18	B	1
4	B	1	19	A	1
5	A	1	20	C	1
6	D	1	21	A	1
7	B	1	22	B	1
8	D	1	23	D	1
9	B	1	24	B	1
10	C	1	25	D	1
11	C	1	26	C	1
12	C	1	27	D	1
13	A	1	28	A	1
14	B	1	29	A	1
15	B	1	30	B	1

YOUR MARKS

Total marks available **30** Your total mark ☐

GUIDELINES - If your mark was:

0 - 8 You need to go over this topic thoroughly; then try again.

9 - 15 Still some weaknesses. Try to identify the places where you are still going wrong.

16 - 22 Not bad; you have reached a good intermediate standard. There are a few improvements that you could make. Have you identified any regular mistakes you were making?

23 - 30 Very good. You are well on top of the essential principles in this area.

COMMENTS

Question

1 Total long-term capital includes debentures as well as share capital and reserves, ie it amounts to £114,000. The profits available to meet the claims of debenture holders and shareholders are the profits before interest and tax, ie £37,000. The ROCE is therefore £37,000/£114,000 or 32.5%.

2

	£
Profit before interest and tax	37,000
Debenture interest	2,000
Profit before tax	35,000
Taxation	9,000
Profit after tax	26,000

This is the amount available for shareholders. Their total capital amounts to £94,000, and so the return on shareholders' capital is £26,000/£94,000 or 27.7%.

3

	£
Profit after tax (see 2 above)	26,000
Preference dividend	1,200
Profits available for equity shareholders	24,800

Equity shareholders' capital consists of share capital (£50,000) plus reserves (£34,000), £84,000 in total. The return on equity shareholders' capital is therefore £24,800/£84,000 = 29.5%.

4 Gearing is defined as the ratio of prior charge capital (here debentures £20,000 plus preference shares £10,000) to total long-term capital (here £114,000). The ratio is therefore £30,000/£114,000 or 26.3%.

5 Earnings are the profits after tax and preference dividends, ie the profits available to ordinary shareholders. The earnings of Barney Ltd amount to £24,800 (see 3 above). The number of shares in issue is 50,000 x 100/25 = 200,000. Earnings per share are therefore £24,800/200,000 = 12.4p.

6 Interest cover measures the extent to which profits before interest and tax are sufficient to meet interest payments owed to loan creditors. Here Barney Ltd has profits before interest and tax of £37,000 and loan interest payable is only £2,000. Interest payments are therefore covered $18\frac{1}{2}$ times (£37,000/£2,000).

Question

7 Preference dividend cover measures the extent to which profit after tax is sufficient to meet dividend payments due to preference shareholders. Here Barney Ltd has a profit after tax of £26,000 (see 2 above) and preference dividends payable are only £1,200. Preference dividends are therefore covered 21.7 times (£26,000/£1,200).

8

ROCE = $\frac{\text{Profit}}{\text{Capital employed}}$

PM = $\frac{\text{Profit}}{\text{Sales}}$

AT = $\frac{\text{Sales}}{\text{Capital employed}}$

It follows that ROCE = PM x AT, which can be re-arranged to the form given in option D.

9 The cash cycle is the length of time between paying for raw materials and receiving cash from the sale of finished goods. In this case Bingo Ltd stores raw materials for three weeks, spends two weeks producing finished goods, four weeks storing the goods before sale and five weeks collecting the money from debtors: a total of 14 weeks. However, six weeks of this period is effectively financed by the company's creditors so that the length of the cash cycle is eight weeks.

10 Examination questions sometimes do not provide all the information that would ideally be needed. In those circumstances you might have to use, for example, the sales figure instead of the cost of sales figure. But in theory the ratio is best calculated using the cost of goods sold.

11 The formula comes from question 10:

$\frac{\text{Cost of goods sold}}{\text{Average stock}}$ = $\frac{£60,000}{£8,000}$

= 7.5 times

COMMENTS

Question

12 The stock turnover period in days is given by the formula:

$$\frac{\text{Average stock}}{\text{Cost of goods sold}} \times 365 \text{ days}$$

Here: $\dfrac{£88,000}{£649,000} \times 365 \text{ days} = 49 \text{ days}$

13 We do not know the average level of debtors during the year because the opening balance is not given. In these circumstances it is necessary to use the closing debtors figure.

The calculation is: $\dfrac{\text{Closing debtors}}{\text{Sales}} \times 365 \text{ days} = 51 \text{ days}.$

14 Again, we must base our calculations on the closing figure for creditors rather than the average figure.

$\dfrac{\text{Closing creditors}}{\text{Purchases}} \times 365 \text{ days} = 47 \text{ days}.$

15

	Current assets £	Current liabilities £
Stock	76,000	
Trade debtors/creditors	120,000	80,000
Prepayments/accruals	8,000	6,000
Cash in hand/overdraft	12,000	16,000
Proposed dividends		10,000
	216,000	112,000

The current ratio is 216:112 = 1.93:1.

16 The quick ratio is calculated in the same way as the current ratio, except that stock is excluded from the total of current assets. The ratio is therefore 140:112 = 1.25:1.

13: ACCOUNTING RATIOS

Question

17

	Days
Stock turnover period (question 12)	49
Debtors collection period (question 13)	_51_
	100
Less creditors payment period (question 14)	_47_
Length of cash cycle	_53_

18

Total long-term capital is £940,000. The profit available to the providers of this capital is the profit before interest and tax, £372,000. The ROCE is therefore £372,000/£940,000 = 39.6%.

19

	£
Profit before interest and tax	372,000
Debenture interest	_6,400_
Profit before tax	365,600
Taxation	_118,000_
Profit after tax	_247,600_

This is the amount available for shareholders. Their total capital amounts to £860,000 and so the return on shareholders' capital is £247,600/£860,000 = 28.8%.

20

	£
Profit after tax (see 19 above)	247,600
Preference dividend	_14,000_
Profit available for equity shareholders	_233,600_

Equity shareholders' capital amounts to £660,000. The return on equity capital is therefore £233,600/£660,000 = 35.4%.

21

Prior charge capital = £280,000
Total long-term capital = £940,000
Gearing ratio = £280,000/£940,000
= 29.8%.

22

Earnings = £233,600 (see 20 above)
Number of ordinary shares in issue = 1,000,000

Earnings per share = £233,600 / 1,000,000
= 23.4p

235

COMMENTS

Question

23 Price per ordinary share = 220p
Earnings per share = 23.4p

Price earnings ratio = $\dfrac{220}{23.4}$

= 9.4

24 The net dividend yield is the amount of dividend per share expressed as a percentage of the share's market value:

$$\dfrac{20p}{220p} \times 100\% = 9.1\%$$

25 $\dfrac{\text{Current assets}}{\text{Current liabilities}} = \dfrac{1.4}{1}$

∴ $\dfrac{\text{Current assets - current liabilities (ie net current assets)}}{\text{Current liabilities}}$

$= \dfrac{1.4 - 1}{1}$

$= \dfrac{0.4}{1}$

∴ Current liabilities $= \dfrac{\text{net current assets}}{0.4}$

$= \dfrac{£64,000}{0.4}$

$= £160,000$

26 The quick ratio is 0.9:1, which means that debtors plus cash are equal to 90% of current liabilities. The current ratio is 1.4:1, which means that stock plus debtors plus cash are equal to 140% of current liabilities. It follows that stock must be equal to 50% of current liabilities, or £80,000.

Question

27
Stock = £80,000 (see 26 above)
Stock turns over 8.775 times per annum
This means that cost of sales = £80,000 x 8.775
= £702,000

Gross profit is 25% of sales
∴ Sales = £702,000 x 100/75
= £936,000

28
Current assets = stock + debtors + bank
Current assets = net current assets + current liabilities
= £64,000 (given) + £160,000 (see 25 above)
= £224,000
Stock = £80,000 (see 26 above)

We can calculate debtors, because we know that they represent six weeks sales. This means that debtors = £936,000 x 6/52 = £108,000.

The formula now becomes:
£224,000 = £80,000 + £108,000 + bank
∴ Bank = £36,000

29
Gross profit = 25% of sales
= 25% x £936,000
= £234,000
Net profit = 40% of share capital
= 40% x £300,000
= £120,000

The difference between these figures is £114,000.

30
Capital and reserves = fixed assets + net current assets.

We know that fixed assets represent 90% of shareholders' funds, so that net current assets must represent the remaining 10%. Fixed assets are therefore nine times as great as net current assets.

Fixed assets = 9 x £64,000
= £576,000
Shareholders' funds = £576,000 + £64,000
= £640,000

Of this total, £300,000 is share capital and £120,000 (see 29 above) is retained profit for the year. The balance (£220,000) must represent retained profits brought forward.

Further information

The Password series includes the following titles:

                                                  Order code

Economics	P01X	EC
Basic accounting	P028	BA
Financial accounting	P036	FA
Costing	P044	CO
Foundation business mathematics	P052	FB
Business law	P060	BL
Auditing	P079	AU
Organisation and management	P087	OM
Advanced business mathematics	P095	AB
Taxation	P109	TX
Management accounting	P117	MA
Interpretation of accounts	P125	IA
Financial management	P133	FM
Company law	P141	CL
Information technology	P15X	IT

Password is available from most major bookshops. If you have any difficulty obtaining them, please contact BPP directly, quoting the above order codes.

                       BPP Publishing Limited
                       Aldine Place
                       142/144 Uxbridge Road
                       London W12 8AA

                       Tel: 01-740 1111
                       Fax: 01-740 1184
                       Telex: 265871 (MONREF G) - quoting '76:SJJ098'